RIDE THE WAVES CREATED BY INSTITUTIONAL INVESTORS

by John Fung

R&E Publishers • **Saratoga, California**

Copyright © 1994 by John T. Fung

All rights reserved.

R & E Publishers
P.O. Box 2008, Saratoga, CA 95070
Tel: (408) 866-6303   Fax: (408) 866-0825

Book Design by Diane Parker
Cover by ASCI, Los Altos, California

Library of Congress Card Catalog Number: 93-87497

ISBN 1-56875-075-7

ACKNOWLEDGMENTS

I wish to express my gratitude to Dr. Earl Cheit, Dean Emeritus, School of Business Administration, University of California at Berkeley, for reviewing the manuscript. Dr. Cheit is a good friend of mine for many years. When I am in doubt about my ability, I always turn to him for advice. His encouragement has helped me achieve many things which I originally thought to be impossible.

I also wish to thank Richard Cheng for his critique on the first draft of the manuscript. An attorney with great interest in the stock market, Richard has identified many loopholes in my reasonings. I am indebted to him for subsequent improvements of the manuscript.

Last but not least, I wish to thank Peter Yu, another stock enthusiast, for his comments from an engineer's perspectives. Peter and I have played the stock game for many years. We have always shared our experiences in dealing with the opportunities and risks of the stock market.

Grateful as I am to my friends for their encouragement and critique, I wish to claim that the ideas and interpretations contained in this book are all mine.

-- John Fung

DEDICATION

To my family, especially Carolyn, Catherine and James.

CONTENTS

STATISTICAL TABLES

1 OPPORTUNITIES AND RISKS

The stock market is a product of the capitalist system. In fact, it is a picture of life itself reflected in the ups and downs of stock prices. All aspects of human nature can be found to play a part in the stock market, such as faith, hope, fear, patience, panic, greed, intrigue, you name it. On top of these, there are the uncontrollable factors like the weather and natural disasters. The uncertainties of world politics and economics always affect the stock market to a great extent. It seems that the odds are too great and the risks too heavy to bear. However, the opportunities are limitless provided one knows how to take advantage of the ups and downs.

Many books have been written about this subject. This book is different in that it provides you with a fresh angle for viewing the market and making investment decisions. The main focus is to understand the stock price movements generated by institutional investors. These are mutual funds, pensions funds, bank trusts, etc. which together account for about 70% of the total volume of stock trade.

No book about the stock market is complete without

examining the behavior of these institutions and their influence on prices. A small investor is always subject to the mercy of the trading practices of these big players. If you ignore them in your investment decisions, you are just groping in the dark and will need tons of luck to pull through.

Chapter 2 will examine the business practices of the institutional investors and their sponsorship of public companies. The communications between the big and small players in the stock market have hardly come under any scrutiny in the past. This chapter will also examine the contents and methods of this information exchange.

In this electronic age, the winner is the one who gets the most relevant information and acts on it fast. The big and small players in the stock market are both exposed to some kind of information. However, the big players can get a little bit more, which in fact is the crucial part that tilts the balance heavily in their favor. The small investors can never hope to obtain the same kind of information available to the big investors. Nevertheless, they can rely on a number of fundamental factors that drive the prices of stocks in the medium to long term. Only in this way can the small investors beat the odds and win.

An attempt is made in Chapter 3 to develop a theory to explain the behavior of institutional investors and their effects on stock prices. How a fund manager handles the investment portfolio is a mystery and therefore a subject of great interest and speculation. The public should not have to wait for the confession of a fund manager to learn the secrets. The reason is that there exist some basic factors that prescribe the business operations of a fund. Chapter 3 will start with the most obvious observations and assumptions, then build on them to arrive at a theory to explain how a fund conducts its business. This theory can also explain the occurrence of a market crash.

Small investors should always exercise caution before committing their money in stocks. However, a bear market or a crash should not become a constant worry. The stock market always recovers after a setback. An economic recession and a market crash are only punctuations in the eternal human quest for a better standard of living. In the human blood, the profit motive is always alive, which is the ultimate unstoppable driving force. There will always be new industries and growth companies. A market crash is a big risk for you to take note and avoid, but a big opportunity for you to take action. Chapter 4 will survey various industries, examine the crucial factors to consider before buying a stock, and identify the opportunities and risks involved.

In order for the profit or loss to be realized in a stock, the investor has to perform two actions: buy and sell (or sell short and buy back). The time between these two actions is a vital part of the game. Once you have put your money into a stock, you are really in business. You will be subject to the fluctuations of the market which may benefit or hurt you. The time you want to get out will determine how much you will win or lose. It can be a very tough and painful decision. It requires some knowledge and discipline that have to be learned and developed.

Chapter 5 will help you formulate a successful investment strategy. The most important thing is to investigate wisely and get into the right stock. Then you will be under less pressure to get out because the stock you have chosen is moving in the direction you expect. You will also learn how to play defensively to conserve capital, and to play aggressively to reap the most profit. This chapter also includes how to insure your investments to protect them from unforeseen circumstances.

Stocks beat other investments because of one great reason: the ease to get in and get out. To invest, you need to put in a relatively small amount of money, with the willingness to take some risks. There is no future commitment whatsoever. You can sell a stock minutes after purchase with no loss incurred. You may even realize some gain. Another great advantage is the ease to expand or contract. You can add or reduce your stock holdings as much and frequent as you want. No other investments offer this kind of flexibility.

Is stock investing a gamble? Yes and no, depending entirely on what you want to do. The same can be said of going into any other business. Risk-taking is the common element involved. The more you know about the business, the less risk you are exposed to. In stocks, if you just go in without much thinking, the game is but a gamble. You may win or lose. However, when you know more about the market and stock selection, the game will become more predictable and financially rewarding.

When you go into a business, you have to sweat it out for a few years to realize some profits. In stocks, you profit not by labor but by the wisdom of buying the income-earning potential of a company (to buy long), or by capitalizing on others' misfortunes (to sell short). This sounds good and cruel, but that is how the world of business works.

The stock market looks very complicated and full of traps. That is why you need to learn how to stay above the inherent confusion and risks. There seem to be a lot of technicalities involved. They only add to the confusion but can do little to help you win in the stock market. As a small investor, all you need is an open mind, some good old common sense, and to value your own experience plus those of others. The purpose of this book is to help you do just that.

2 THE BIG INVESTORS

The stock market is only a place where people trade pieces of paper called stocks, despite all the myth and technicalities surrounding it. If you want to be a player, it is very important to know who you are dealing with. It is also important to understand the behavior of other players in the game. The players can be divided into two groups: the institutions and the small investors. The former consist of mutual funds, pensions funds, insurance companies, brokerage firms, bank trusts, etc. The latter consist of people like you and me.

Investing institutions in America number by the thousands, many with assets worth several billion dollars or more. Among them, the mutual funds have gained enormous popularity. The number of mutual funds alone already exceeds 3,000 nowadays. The institutional investors dominate the market by virtue of their trading volumes, widely estimated around 70% of the total stock trade.

THE PRICE MOVERS

Independent small investors do not buy or sell a given stock at the same time. So their combined volume of trade cannot affect the direction of the market. One exception is panic sell or frantic buy. This happens under two conditions. One is the arrival of some shocking news. The other is a response to a surprisingly big movement of the market initiated by some big investors. Sometimes, small investors can even be orchestrated to respond in a desired fashion.

Since the stock price is determined by supply and demand at a particular time, an institution which tenders a large quantity for sale or buy can influence the stock price in either direction. Price manipulation can easily be done during the opening or closing hours of the trading day when most people are not ready or tired of responding. A relatively small volume can make a big price movement. That is why program trades done by big investors usually occur during these times.

Program trades execute all at once market orders of 1,000 shares or more in up to 200 different Blue Chip stocks in the New York Stock Exchange. The orders are either all buys or all sells. The result will bring an immediate significant movement of the Dow Jones Industrial Average which comprises only 30 Blue Chip stocks. One or a combination of the following motives are involved in a program trade: profit taking, loss minimizing, price manipulation, or communicating to the world about the mood of the stock market.

The big investors hold all the good cards in the game. If they refuse to sell their big holdings of a stock, the price cannot collapse. If they embark on continuous buying, the price can jump to unbelievable levels. Should they choose to dump, it would look as if the end of the world is near. This is in fact the real-life situation on Wall Street. For small investors, you have to appreciate the great influence of the institutions on stock prices. You must think about their possible actions every time you make a move. While they make waves, you just have to swim with the waves.

COMMUNICATIONS BETWEEN PLAYERS

The flow of information is very crucial for stock market players. It takes various forms. Some information is extremely relevant. The great majority can be interpreted either way. The small investors usually get those which are subject to interpretation. When they get the most relevant information, it is usually late. At worst, they may get misleading information which causes a financial loss.

Let us examine the sources and contents of the information flowing to the small investors. There are four basic sources: media, professionals, acquaintances, and direct experience. The media consist of newspapers, financial journals, regular company reports, television, radio, and the rather recent addition of personal computer network.

Professionals consist of stockbrokers, analysts, and seminars conducted by specialists. Acquaintances can be anybody you know or come into contact with. Direct experience consists of the lessons you have learned the hard way. Some investors like to test out the products before they buy the stock of a company.

The contents of information flowing to the small investors range from gossip to very technical analysis. They cover market trends, new products, company reports, Wall Street news, etc. The problems facing the small investors are as follows:

First, the quantity of information is huge and diverse. Due to time limit, the small investors can only see a minute portion which they are exposed to. Therefore they tend to lack a balanced view, or miss the point altogether.

Second, only a few crucial factors have direct connections with the stock price. They are not hard to identify but are usually buried under the myriad of less relevant data. The crucial factors will be examined later in this chapter and in Chapter 4.

Third, some news may receive much more attention than they deserve, such as new products, management changes, companies forming an alliance, etc. These news usually push up the stock price and fuel speculation. How long can the news sustain the stock price? Can the companies involved produce greater profits because of those news? Some encouraging news may turn out to be the harbinger of a stock's doomsday. A company's new products have yet to generate enough revenue to cover the costs, beat the competition in the marketplace, improve the balance sheet of the company, and most importantly, impress Wall Street.

What kind of information is flowing to the big investors? Suppose Jim is portfolio manager of a big fund. He is exposed to the same kind of information as are small investors. However, if he bases his investment decisions only on those information, he will lose his job the next day. The reason is that as a big player, he has access to the most relevant information denied to small investors.

If Jim has doubts about a company's performance or future plans, he just makes an appointment to see the Chief Executive or the Chief Financial Officer. They will be more than happy to see him, because without institutional sponsorship, the company's stock is going nowhere. By discussing with the top officers, hc will be able to put the company in proper perspectives. He will be able to assess how much the various products of the company contribute to total profit and cost; how much the customers like the products; who are the competitors and what are their impacts; what is the price trend which will affect profit margin; and so on. If he is only a few weeks from the release of the next quarterly report, he can just ask to take a peek at the intermediate financial results. This will give him a tremendous advantage over small investors.

If Jim's fund has a big holding in the company, it pays

to find out who are the other big investors because their decisions affect him and vice versa. This can be done through the major brokerage houses, the stock exchanges, or simply the big players' regular cocktail party. He has to know the portfolio managers of other big funds. He touches base with them frequently to check out their views and concerns.

On a daily basis, Jim finds out from the stock exchanges or the brokerage houses where the big orders are coming from, how the orders are queued up on both buy and sell sides, and so on. He will also find out what the small investors as a group are doing by routinely contacting his friends at the stock exchanges or brokerage firms. He may be surprised by the large volume of short selling done by the small investors on a stock, which constitutes a big pent-up demand for they have to buy back the stock eventually. If he boosts up the price, the short-sellers will scramble to buy back to minimize their losses, which will send the price even higher. At that time Jim then starts to sell.

Jim is aware of the government regulations restricting his practices as a fund manager, but what he is doing is within legal limits. Most importantly, he gets the most relevant information, makes the best decision, and reaps a great profit.

Now let us examine communications between major players and small players. The stock trades which the small investors have completed are available as records for odd (small) lots. The trades they intend to do at given prices are also available as limit orders placed. The stock options on record reflect the general view of small investors regarding the price directions of stocks. As described earlier, the short selling done is also available on the records of brokerage houses.

All of these information represent a show of cards by the small investors without their knowing about it. The big investors only need to tap into the brokerage firms or the stock exchanges. They will respond accordingly for their own benefits. On the other hand, similar information about what the big investors are doing are hardly available to the small investors. Hence the flow of information in the trading aspect is unidirectional.

Outside of actual stock trade, there is a huge flow of information from the big investors to the public. This includes analyses of the stock market, of products, industries and companies. The institutions are more than happy to supply the less relevant information to the public, for a price of course.

As the stock market grows, there is an accompanying explosion of information. This is enhanced to a great extent by telecommunications, computers and network systems. The market becomes more sophisticated and responses are much faster. However, it still remains a wild beast, always full of surprises. The desire of the public to learn more about this increasingly technical yet mysterious market creates a fertile ground for a big business enterprise. Thus we have analysts, financial consultants and other specialists coming in, trying to make sense and profits out of the huge pool of data available. Their productions consist of analyst's reports, financial journals, Wall Street programs on television, etc.

The big investors are quick to take advantage of this information explosion. They can collect the statistics much easier for their own use. They can invent more indices and formulas to describe the market. They can recompile the statistics to attract more readership. They can interprete the figures in whatever way they like. Finally, they can sell their productions to the public.

If you look at the employers of the stock analysts and other related professionals, how many are self-employed and truly independent? Most of them work under the tutelage of big players like mutual funds and brokerage firms. They are actually playing the role of technical writers disseminating information from the big players to the general public.

A big player can easily undermine the credibility of a prominent analyst recommending a stock for buy by dumping the very same stock the next day. However, big players have every reason to promote the credibility of the analysts they hire. This huge information market hinges on the credibility of those who interpret the statistics. If the analysts lose their credibility, the information market cannot realize its full potential which has benefited the big players so much already.

The analysts also fulfill another function for the big players. If the big players want to support the price of a given stock, continuous buying using their own money may prove to be too expensive. They need additional capital from the small investors. How can they talk to the millions of them out there? An optimistic analyst's report, coupled with Wall Street news about other analysts upgrading the stock, will do the trick.

Analysts' reports are generally credible and fun to read. Forecasts and predictions down to the industry level are usually correct. However, at the company level, small investors must be very careful about the interpretations, which are worded to protect the authors' credibility and promote their objectives. When an analyst recommends a buy. It means a lot of things. It may mean that the stock price is on the rise. It may mean that the company's prospects still look good. It may mean that the employer of the analyst has already bought a lot of shares and therefore the stock must be good. It may mean that only the industry is good which should benefit the company regardless of the competition. The small investors are given all the freedom to choose which one to believe.

INSTITUTIONAL RISKS

Institutional investors have their own problems and frustrations. Despite close contacts with top officers of the companies they own, they are usually unable to exercise due power as major investors. This is now changing. Major investors will gradually play a bigger role in top management decisions of public companies.

An institution's biggest worry is unwise strategic decisions made by individual companies. After a few years of good earnings, a successful company has accumulated a lot of cash and substantial institutional sponsorship. The urge to expand and diversify is hard to resist. Thus the company goes out to to find a merger, buy another company, or venture into a new business. If this turns out to be a failure, it will certainly affect profits and stock prices for years to come.

There are government and security exchange regulations restricting the practices of institutional investors. One of them forbids an institution to hold more than a certain percentage of the total outstanding shares of a company. This percentage is known to be around ten percent. Although this regulation puts a limit on the dominance of an institution in a stock, only a handful of institutions each holding the maximum limit can effectively control the price of the stock. Moreover, ten percent is a very large quantity compared with the average trading volume of a stock, which seldom exceeds one percent of the total outstanding shares in a single day.

Competition among big investors seems to be on the rise due to the increasing number of mutual funds. The consequence is that price support for a given stock may get more costly and unpredictable as the institutions try to undercut each other. However, this trend may not be happening due to several reasons enumerated below.

The number of American public companies now stands at 5,000 and growing, effectively widening the investment target range. The new mutual funds tend to specialize in a wider variety of investments such as growth stocks, low capitalization stocks, foreign stocks, etc. Thus the likelihood of many institutions crowding into a few stocks is reduced.

Finally, this kind of business emphasizes on maximum returns for investors in a specific area of investment. Unlike other business, there is no need to capture a great market share by undercutting the competitors.

Therefore, it is expected that the institutions would rather consult than undercut one another. Chapter 3 will further discuss this aspect of institutional cooperation.

INSTITUTIONAL HOLDINGS

Institutional investors play the stock market for a living. They are well dug in for the long haul. After a market crash, many small investors will leave, but the institutions will stay and will be organizing a future rally. In general, institutional investors are stable, conservative, and hence predictable in the medium to long term.

In the business world, small companies come and go. Institutions are reluctant to bet on those companies. They prefer to invest in established industries and companies with a long track record of stability. No doubt, they always keep an eye on growth industries and promising companies. When a growth company has demonstrated a string of impressive earnings, the institutions will enter in full force.

Institutions also like to diversify their portfolios to protect themselves against industry decline and under-performing companies. Furthermore, maintaining the major bulk of investment in a diversity of well-established companies serves as a good selling point. An investor will not like to join a mutual fund if the prospectus shows the fund's portfolio consisting of small and unknown companies.

Table 2-1 shows institutional holdings in top companies in their respective industries.

Table 2-1: Institutional Holdings in Leading Companies of Various Industries.

Companies	Sales '92 $ billions	Institutional Holdings (%) 1991	1993	Share Prices ($) Oct.91 High	Feb.93 High	Profits 1992 $ millions
General Motors	132.8	38	40	38 7/8	41 1/4	-23,498
Exxon	103.5	38	40	61 7/8	64 7/8	+ 4,770
IBM	65.1	49	45	1393/4	54 7/8	- 4,965
AT&T	65.1	31	34	39 1/2	56 1/2	+3,807
General Electric	62.2	51	54	77 5/8	87 3/4	+4,725
Sears Roebuck	59.1	58	60	39 1/8	54 3/4	-3,932
Philip Morris	50.2	61	59	74 5/8	77 5/8	+4,939
DuPont	37.6	39	41	50	50	-3,927
Citicorp	36.0*	50	50	17 1/2	27 5/8	+722
Boeing	30.2	46	42	53	40 7/8	+552
Procter & Gamble	29.9	44	46	†45 1/8	54	+1,872
Pepsico	22.1	56	57	35 5/8	42 1/2	+374
Eastman Kodak	20.6	52	58	47 1/4	54 1/4	+1,146
Dow Chemical	19.2	50	54	58	59 3/8	-489
Hewlett-Packard	16.4	50	55	51 5/8	76	+549
AMR	14.5	84	83	65 3/4	65 7/8	-935
Digital Equipment	14.0	68	65	65	49 1/4	-2,796
Minnesota Mining	13.9	64	66	97 1/2	109 3/4	+1,233
Johnson & Johnson	13.8	51	58	†50 1/8	50 3/8	+1,030
International Paper	13.6	65	59	78 1/4	69 7/8	+86
Tenneco	13.6	48	59	52	47	-1,323
Time Warner	13.1	37	68	†23	35 5/8	+86
Fleming	12.9	75	85	36 1/4	34 3/8	+113
Goodyear Tire	11.9	59	75	50 5/8	75	-659
Bristol-Myers Squ.	11.8	59	53	81 1/2	60 3/8	+1,962
Aluminum Co.	9.6	73	77	73 1/8	78 7/8	-1,139
Marriott	8.9	35	38	17 1/4	24 5/8	+85
Waste Management	8.7	50	52	38 1/4	39 7/8	+850
Walt Disney	7.6	40	41	†30	47 7/8	+817
Humana	6.9	72	75	30 5/8	21 3/8	+122
Fluor	6.7	63	54	45 5/8	45 3/8	+6
Capital Cities/ABC	5.4	80	80	434 1/2	514	+246

Sources: Standard & Poor's Stock Guide, Fortune Magazine.
† Adjusted for splits   *Estimate

Table 2-1 provides some insight into institutional holdings in the common stocks of big companies. It appears that there is not much correlation between holdings and profits. The reasoning is that the institutions go into a top company for the long term because of its size, clout and dividend payments. As long as there are satisfactory profits and dividends, it pays to stay put and support the price. If a loss occurs in one year or two, it does not justify an exodus because big companies do not go away so easily. Some examples are General Motors, Sears, Du Pont, Tenneco, Goodyear Tire, and Aluminum Co. of America, where institutional holdings actually increased when large losses were incurred.

In the case of IBM, the stock price has dropped by more than half due to a combination of big losses, uncertain future for mainframe computers, and speculation about reduced dividends. However, institutional holding came down by a comparatively small amount. Digital Equipment is another electronic giant which incurred big losses but only a small decrease in institutional holdings. In the case of a big drug company like Bristol-Myers Squibb, the stock price and institutional holdings dropped in the presence of an excellent profit. This is due to uncertainties associated with health care reforms initiated by the Clinton Administration.

With respect to the relationship between holdings and prices, the stock price certainly goes up when big investors buy more. An institution usually buys more in a big company when the stock price comes under downward pressure. The reasons are two-fold. One is to arrest the declining value of their existing holdings. The other is to take advantage of a price dip in preparation for a rally later. Citicorp is a good case in point. During 1991, the stock price has steadily come down from around $17 to $9 in the winter. The bank had a large inventory of problem loans and was in the process of cleaning up and reorganizing. The institutions did not reduce their holdings of around 50% despite the price drop. They sold the stock and bought it back at lower prices.

In late December, the Federal Reserve cut the interest rate by one point which ushered a bull market that continued into 1993. The lower interest rate helped a lot of banks by reducing their costs of operations. In mid-January 1992, the price of Citicorp shot up to $15 in three consecutive days. This was probably due to institutional scrambling to buy the stock at low prices. The price continued to rise since then. During the first few months of 1993, the price of Citicorp followed a cyclical pattern between the range of $25 and $30. After the rebound, the institutional holding of Citicorp still hovers around 50 percent, which seems like a saturation point for this company. Chapter 3 will offer a theory to explain the relationship between institutional holdings and stock price movements.

Stability characterizes institutional holdings of big companies. This stability decreases with the size of the company because smaller companies usually carry more risks in the competitive business environment. Table 2-2 shows institutional holdings in medium-size companies in various industries.

Table 2-2: Institutional Holdings in Selected Medium-Size Companies

Companies	Institutional Holdings (%)		Share Prices ($)		Profits
			Oct.91	Feb.93	1992
	1991	1993	High	High	$ millions
Western Digital	25	23	3 3/8	9 5/8	-73
Dell Computer	35	48	35 1/4	49 1/8	+51
SCI Systems	62	79	7 3/4	23	+4
Nortek	23	32	1 /78	6 1/8	-24
Maxtor	28	54	5 5/8	11 3/8	+7
Magma Copper	56	29	7	18 5/8	+55
Eagle-Pitcher Ind.	11	8	1 7/8	5 1/2	+29
Vishay Intertech.	37	49	19	37 1/4	+30
Applied Materials	79	89	28 1/4	40 1/4	+40
Harman Intl. Ind.	39	58	10 1/8	18	+4
Giddings & Lewis	83	96	30 3/8	29 1/2	+36
Hudson Foods	8	7	9	14 7/8	+2
Doskocil	3	37	1 1/8	16 1/2	-27
Fisher-Price	2	55	30 3/4	29 1/4	+41
Banta	70	72	28 1/4	46 1/4	+36
Cisco	81	90	49 1/2	94 1/4	+81*
Cabletron Syst.	29	46	52 1/2	90 1/2	+58
Synoptics	73	82	24	93 1/4	+40*
Informix	27	79	15 3/8	41	+54*
Oracle Systems	29	49	16 1/8	34 1/2	+61*
Borland Intl.	37	74	67 3/4	22 1/8	-110

Sources: Standard & Poor's Stock Guide, Fortune Magazine

* Estimates

Table 2-2 gives a list of companies with annual sales of $1 billion or less, which have provided high returns to investors in 1992. For most of these companies, institutional holdings vary over a wide range during a short period of about a year. This means that due to the risk factor, institutions are very sensitive to the quarterly performance of smaller companies. They will adjust their holdings quickly once the revenues and profits become known. When the institutional holding increases significantly, an impressive rise in the stock price will follow, as shown by Informix, Doskocil, SCI Systems, and some others in Table 2-2. The reverse will also apply if these companies do not perform to expectations.

There are quite a few companies where institutional holdings reach a very high percentage, such as Giddings & Lewis, Cisco, Synoptics and Applied Materials. Such high holdings signify the bright prospects of these companies as viewed by the institutions. The big investors have already positioned themselves for further rises in the stock prices. Very likely this will be accompanied by stock splits. One notable exception is Borland where a stock price decline is accompanied by an increase in institutional holdings. This may suggest that the lowest price level has been reached where the institutions have already begun to accumulate the stock in anticipation of a rebound.

PRICE MOVEMENTS

Institutional decisions regarding their holdings can explain a lot about the movements of stock prices. Suppose Mary is a portfolio manager of a big fund. The fund has an existing diversity of stock holdings. She cannot just keep her fund's holdings and hope to make a profit out of it. She has to buy and sell on a daily basis according to the opportunities that come along. As a big player and a leader, she knows that not only must she chase after opportunities, but also make them happen in the stock market. She may not have total control over the bulls and bears, but certainly she can delay and prolong their comings and goings.

What are her risks? Well, she does not feel comfortable if she has bought and is still holding onto a stock at too high a price. The price is basically what she wants to support according to the performance of the company and market conditions in a particular time frame. There is no such thing as a market price which she should accept. She can move the price in either direction if she has enough leverage. Her leverage consists of two things: a large stock holding at a price well below the current market level, and plenty of cash ready to buy. The former enables her to dump the stock without suffering a loss. The latter enables her to continue to raise the price.

Suppose the stock price of a mid-size company now stands at $25. The total shares outstanding number 50 million, of which her fund holds 5 million. Of course she did not buy all of them at one time. She purchased 3 million shares a year ago within a two-month period between $7 and $10 per share. She knows that her actions at that time excited the market and initiated the surge of the company's stock to the current level. From $10 onward, she played the ups and downs of the stock with the objective to boost the price to over $20 within a year. That means within this period, she bought more than she sold thus she wound up with an additional holding of 2 million shares between $10 and $25 a share.

She knows that she cannot go beyond the legal limit of ten percent of the company's total outstanding shares. Furthermore, she found out recently that there were plenty of ready sellers whenever she attempted to buy some more. Hence it is getting increasingly expensive to support the price. The stock market now presents some new opportunities in another industry, which outshine the prospects of the company in question. A combination of these factors leads her to decide to switch.

There are only a handful of big players with holdings about the same size as hers. She spends some time sounding out her plan to the other big players to find out their possible reactions. This kind of consultation is necessary for the sake of reciprocity. Within a day or two, the final decision to switch is reached.

She has to give an excuse for the planned exodus. To find an excuse is never difficult. She has to prepare the market for the impending sell. She gathers the analysts for a conversation. If she is kind-hearted, she expresses her concerns about the stock to give the public some warning. If she is cold-blooded, she just expresses optimism to encourage more buyers. The next day, she carries out her plan to sell while monitoring the situation. Her actions generate the same kind of commotion as she did a year ago, except in the opposite direction. She initiates the sell, the small investors follow when they see the big drop in prices. Within a month or so, the stock price comes down to $5. She has completed the exodus with more cash in hand than she began a year ago. The price may drop some more if no other big players want to support it.

She moves on to open another gold mine in another industry. If things do not work out, she is always welcome back to the same company. This time it will be even cheaper to hold an initial 3 million shares. This case is a planned surge for the stock she sponsored a year ago, and a planned crash which she has just engineered. The whole cycle nets her more cash and a chance to begin all over again at a lower cost. The real situation may not be this simple as described. On the way down, if the other big players feel bullish about the stock, she will have an easy sell. If they feel the same way, it will be an exodus coordinated between the big players, resulting in lesser profit and a bigger drop in the stock price.

IMPLICATIONS FOR SMALL INVESTORS

Small investors should never assume that perfect competition exists in the stock market. It is an entirely different market dominated by big players and clouded by the huge flow of information which confuses more than enlightens. The market price of a stock does not reflect the real worth of a company. It only reflects the future of the company as seen by institutional investors. The market price of a stock is based on demand and supply at a particular time. It is a true market price for the small investors because they have no control and have to accept it. On the other hand, the big investors never accept the market price because they know that they are in a position to influence its direction.

The flow of information in the stock market is really lopsided. The most relevant information goes to the big players while the huge remainder goes to the public. To make matters worse, very little information going to the public is directly related to the stock price, and most of it is subject to interpretation. If small investors make their decisions based on this kind of information, they will need a lot of luck to win. The best way is to look for some crucial indicators that determine the stock price, then monitor the results as the market goes. The chapters that follow will examine those crucial factors in more details.

3 INSTITUTIONAL INVESTOR'S BEHAVIOR:
A General Theory

This chapter attempts to develop a simple theory to explain the behavior of institutional investors such as mutual funds. The purpose is to try to understand their motives and actions. Once we know more about their behavior, we can better explain the movements of stock prices and stay above the confusion inherent in the stock market.

BASIC ASSUMPTIONS

Although it remains a great mystery as to how the institutions manage their investment portfolios, the following observations are reasonable and beyond doubt:

- A mutual fund exists for the purpose of making a profit just like any other business. It does not intend to cash out and disappear the next day like some small investors do. It plans to stay and grow, therefore it must set its eyes on the long term.

- The funds compete among themselves to attract investors' money just like the banks do. While the banks emphasize on service and convenience, the funds stress on performance and dividends.

- The security of investment is an important factor for attracting customers. While the banks emphasize their long years of existence, the funds cannot boast a long company history. The banks' assets such as loans and real estates have much more stable values compared to the funds' holdings of stocks which may depreciate a large percentage in a single day.

- Both banks and funds review their assets regularly based on changing market conditions. The funds do their reviews much more often due to the volatility of the stock market. Just holding on the assets is a very dangerous practice because they may evaporate quickly. Therefore, unprofitable or depreciating assets have to be sold and cheaper assets of higher potential have to be added. Both banks and funds are constantly engaging in maintaining and increasing their asset values.

- Although the stock market has rules and regulations protecting the small investors and restricting the practices of the funds, the fluctuation of a stock price reflects the confluence of supply and demand at a particular moment of time. A large quantity of stock for buy or sell at one time has much greater effect on the price than many small quantities spread over the entire trading day.

- The flow of information in the stock market is almost instantaneous thanks to telecommunications and computer systems. However, the contents of information exchanged between different types of players are not the same. Chapter 2 already described some of the information not available to small investors.

Having set forth all the above as basic assumptions, we can now proceed to develop the following theory.

LONG-TERM STOCK HOLDINGS

A mutual fund always keeps a certain amount of idle cash for redemptions demanded by investors. When the market looks bad, the amount of idle cash will be increased. During a market crash, a mutual fund may be forced to sell some of its stock holdings at a loss to satisfy a sudden surge in redemptions.

The total asset value of a mutual fund depends on two basic things: the quantities of different stocks it owns, and the current market prices of those stocks. A fund manager has a nightmare if the majority of the holdings were bought at current market prices. The manager gets nervous if the gaps between the current market prices and the costs of the fund's stocks are narrowing. It is a very important objective for the fund manager to widen this price gap. How can that be accomplished?

A fund must allocate a significant portion of its cash to buy stocks of well-established companies. This investment is also diversified to cover as many industries as possible. We can conveniently call this the core portfolio (or core investment). This represents an asset to be held for the long term. The size of this asset varies depending on the circumstances. The core portfolio serves a number of purposes. First, it provides security because well-established companies normally have stable earnings hence relatively stable stock prices. Second, most of these companies pay dividends. Third, the core portfolio serves as a selling point to attract more investors.

It would be ideal to hold the core portfolio at low prices both for protection and leverage. For an older mutual fund, the core investment probably costs a small percentage of its current market value. The reason is that the fund has started accumulating the core portfolio many years ago when the prices were low. The quantity of this core investment has also multiplied due to stock splits.

For a mutual fund recently formed, it costs much more to start a core portfolio of well-established companies at current market prices. It is better to concentrate on smaller growth companies whose stocks it can accumulate at low prices. For this reason, old and new mutual funds have different target companies as far as core investment goes. This also explains the fact that many new mutual funds are specializing in growth, low capitalization, and other types of low-price stocks. This does not mean that the older funds cannot do a good job. In fact, the older funds are constantly adding growth companies to their core portfolios because growth companies have the prospects of becoming future giants.

When a core-portfolio company fails the expected performance for successive quarters, the funds will gradually reduce the concentration of this company in the core portfolio, resulting in a stock price drop. When the worst is almost over where the price stays at a low level, the funds will begin to accumulate the stock to bring it back to a desired level in the core portfolio. The new mutual funds also see this as an opportunity to accumulate the stocks of a well-established company at a low price. Thus it may result in a scramble for the stock. That is why a big company rebound always propels the stock price fast initially, then steadily onward to the previous high level.

Sometimes the price drop of a core-portfolio company is not performance related. It may be due to a war, an uncertainty situation, or a general market crash which triggers a big selling. After the event, the funds will come back quickly and replenish their core stocks at low prices. The lowest price at which the funds start to replenish their long-term holdings can be considered as the support price of the stock.

REVENUES GENERATION

It is obvious that just holding onto the core stocks makes no profit except the dividend payments. Selling the core stocks generates income but it requires replenishment which may never be done at the original low prices. Therefore, a mutual fund has to buy low and sell high frequently at current market prices to generate revenues.

A significant portion of the total cash has to be set aside for revenue generation on a daily basis. A mutual fund likes to trade the stocks of its core portfolio for it has more leverage on the price. It can move the price up by heavy buying. It can also move it down by dumping from its large core portfolio.

Selling from the core portfolio is only done when the stock's long-term prospects appear uncertain. With plenty of cash available, the best way for a fund to play the market is to lead the stock price in a cyclical movement well above the core portfolio cost. This explains why most big company stocks are moving in an up-and-down cycle within certain limits.

The psychology of the stock market makes it possible for the cyclical pattern to continue. Unlike the car market for example, if a dealer raises the price, consumers will be encouraged to switch to other competitors, thus exerting a downward pressure on the price. In the stock market, when a stock price goes up, people expect more profits, so they jump in. Hence a fund just needs to buy heavily to raise the price to attract the attention of other investors. When they join in, lifting the price higher, then the fund begins to sell, thus depressing the price and enabling it to restart the cycle once again. The fund does not have to sell from the core portfolio. It just cashes out its investment made to boost up the price a few days ago. This pattern can be maintained to go on and on.

The following diagram illustrates this point:

	Cyclical high $70	-----------------------
Market price range		
	Cyclical low $60	Fund's minority holding is within this price spread
Market buffer		
	Core-holding high $30	-----------------------
		Fund's majority holding is within this price spread
Original cost of stock		
	Core-holding low $5	---------------------

For most well-established companies, the market price of the stock moves cyclically within relatively narrow limits. In the diagram above, let's say the cyclical limits are between $60 and $70. The fund holds a few million shares of this company in the core portfolio accumulated when the price ranged between $5 and $30. This is the ideal situation because there is a significant price gap or market buffer of $30 between the core-holding high and the cyclical low. The market buffer represents some kind of a comfort zone.

There should be no incentive to decrease the core holding unless a collapse is expected in the market price. The income derived from this stock has two components:

the dividend payments of the core holding, and the profits generated from frequent buys and sells within the cyclical market price range.

There are all kinds of market condition that cause the cyclical low to move closer to the core-holding high, thus reducing the market buffer. When this happens, the fund manager must decide whether to buy to widen the buffer, or to sell the stock from the core portfolio. If the manager judges that the prospects of the company are still good and that the price dip is only a temporary phenomenon, then it is better to buy and raise the market price. Otherwise, a sell from the core portfolio will be made resulting in further declines of the price.

To generate the ups and downs of the stock price, the funds move cash in and out of different companies on a daily basis. The funds also do the same thing from one industry to another in response to news and market conditions. These are the waves created by the funds. Once a small investor gets into the market, he or she has to follow the waves quickly. A small investor can ignore the waves if the stock was bought at a price low enough around the support level, that is between the core-holding high and low.

The funds are eager to influence the decisions of small investors because they need outside capital to play the stock game. Therefore we have a respected profession consisting of analysts and other specialists to communicate with the public. A discussion of stock player communications has been given in Chapter 2.

We have covered the case of cyclical price movements of well-established companies. As for medium to small companies, the behavior of the funds is less predictable because the market buffer is small or even non-existent.

The following diagram illustrates this point:

———————————————	Market high $20 (may go higher)
Market price range so far this year	
———————————————	Market low $10 (may fall below $2)
Market buffer	
———————————————	Holding high $8
Original cost of stock	
———————————————	Holding low $2

Smaller companies do not have huge resources to cushion the impacts of bad times. Therefore it is more risky to hold their stocks. In the diagram above, the fund has not decided yet to keep the company in its core portfolio pending evaluation of more quarterly earnings. At the present time, the market is good for the company as the price ranges between $10 and $20. The company went public three years ago with an initial offering of $5 per share. The fund has been playing this stock since then. The company has some good potentials, hence the fund has accumulated one million shares between $2 and $8.

Because small company stocks are volatile, the market

buffer is small with a gap of only $2. The fund manager is keeping a close eye on this company. If the performance falls below expectation for the first time, the fund will initiate a big sell to protect itself. If the prospects of the company turn ugly, the fund will dispose of all its holding, which may drive the price to below $2.

Many growth stocks have matured and become long-term holdings of the core portfolios of mutual funds. The following scenerio is commonly seen. A company has shown good growths in both sales and profits for quite some time. The funds have accumulated significant holdings of the stock, resulting in a steady price upsurge. Then a stock split follows, doubling the quantity of the funds' holdings at the original cost. This means that the average cost per share is now reduced to half. At the same time, the market price of the stock is also reduced to half after the split. The lower price now makes it less costly for the funds to continue more buying until the price is raised to a desired level. Additional splits may follow and the process repeats itself. In this way, the market buffer is widened, the core portfolio has more shares of the company, and the stock is launched to the normal cyclical pattern characteristic of a well-established company.

COMPETITION BETWEEN MUTUAL FUNDS

A survey of mutual funds reveals an interesting fact. There are only a few new funds which have succeeded in establishing themselves in the stock trading business on their own. Most of the new funds are actually created as spin-offs from well-established funds. If a big old fund spins off a few new ones, there is no reason to assume that the new funds are created to directly compete with the parent.

A new fund is created most likely for the following purposes. First, the new fund will attract more customers by capitalizing on the parent's clout and specializing in another type of investment different from that of the parent. Second, the new fund will take on a higher risk of investing in new opportunities without directly affecting the performance of the parent fund. Third, it costs a lot more for the new fund to start building a core portfolio of well-established companies at current market prices. The most cost-effective way to start a new fund is to accumulate the low-price stocks of growth companies. Besides this, the stocks of growth companies usually split a few times, thereby multiplying the quantities of the fund's holdings.

With respect to the ease of entry into the fund business, a survey of mutual funds suggests that entry is difficult without parental sponsorship. This is shown by the predominance of new funds which are created under the old funds' umbrellas. Table 3-1 illustrates the competitive situation between mutual funds. It is apparent that the market is dominated by a handful of funds with huge asset values. These leading funds have created many new ones forming diversified financial groups covering all types of investment opportunities.

**Table 3-1. Leading Mutual Funds and Their
Sponsorship of Newer Funds**

Fund Groups	Net Asset of Biggest Fund Within Each Group ($Billion) 3/31/93	Number of Other Funds In Same Group
Vanguard	97.6	13
Fidelity	24.9	26
American Funds	16.9	21
Franklin	14.1	44
Janus	7.3	2
Kemper	6.9	13
IDS	6.3	8
Putnam	6.2	31
20th Century	5.7	3
AIM Weingarten	5.6	7
Dean Witter	5.6	20
Dreyfus	4.3	5
Pioneer	4.3	10
Templeton	4.2	4
Lord Abbett	3.9	10
Prudential	3.9	5
Fortress	3.7	2
Van Kampen	3.6	6
American Capital	3.6	8
Colonial	3.3	18
Financial Industrial	3.3	1
Mutual Shares	3.2	1
Nicholas	3.0	1

Source: Standard & Poor's Stock Guide, May 1993

If the parent fund and its own spin-offs do not compete with each other, does the parent fund compete with other parents and other spin-offs? This depends on two things: the nature of the business and the practices of the fund managers. In this business environment, the investment target range is ever broadening due to more companies going public and new industries emerging. The funds always have a wider variety of companies to choose from. By concentrating investments in a fair number of companies, each fund can become a dominant player in its own territory without colliding head-on with other funds.

The nature of this business is characterized by heavy emphasis on performance. The customers only demand highest returns for their money without questioning how the funds manage their assets. The pursuit of a greater market share is irrelevant and therefore unnecessary. A fund only wants to be a dominant sponsor of a stock so that it is in a position to lead the up-and-down cycles and to profit by generating these waves. A fund never wants to have the entire market and become the sole player of a stock, for who will buy its shares when it wants to cash out? The normal situation would be for a few funds to dominate the trading of the stock. One fund takes its turn to generate a wave while the others cooperate by not under-cutting its effort. The small investors are of course in the dark as to what is happening. They just play catchup with the waves.

The trading practices of the funds are a great mystery

that fuels a lot of speculation. They deserve close examination if we want to make some sense out of the ups and downs of the stock market. To examine the trading practices of the funds, we need to think about how the fund managers communicate with one another. We cannot assume that the managers of the mutual funds do not talk to one another. Nor should we be surprised if they are good friends. Although government regulations forbid unfair practices, they cannot forbid the fund managers to attend cocktail parties, to play golf together, or to invite each other over for dinner, where business deals are usually made.

The cooperation between the funds ultimately depends on how much the managers want to compromise their self-interests. One thing understood by all is that if the stock price does not move, nobody will make any profit, including the small investors. A big player has to make the first move to stir the market and the other big players should not neutralize its effort. This kind of understanding can be achieved by consultation among the major players before any wave is due to start. When the present wave subsides, another major player will take its turn. In this way, the ball is passed on from one big player to another, and the waves continue from one company or industry to another.

The funds do not want to compete head-on with one another in daily trading of stocks. However, they must compete to attract the small investors' money to increase the cash inflow. As more funds are being formed, small investors are given more choices. Many funds offer no fees and no restrictions for joining and redeeming, which means that small investors can switch between funds as often as they please. This will eventually force the funds to keep a bigger percentage of their holdings in cash to satisfy unpredictable redemptions. More idle cash to meet redemptions means less money flowing to the stock trade. It does not mean that the funds are losing their influence on stock prices.

The stock market is far from perfect competition. The market is dominated by several huge funds with tremendous resources to make waves. Although the number of funds has increased dramatically, the steady expansion of the big funds into other areas by spining off newer funds do not add to the competition environment.

At one extreme where only one fund dominates the stock, the market resembles a monopoly. In cases where there are only a handful of dominant players, close consultation between the funds may result in an outright collusion. In the case of a well-established company with several hundred million shares issued and sponsored by several hundred funds, the market is still far from perfect competition. The reason is the ability of some big players to make waves. Consequently, the direction of the market is controlled by a few leaders holding the most shares. All the other major players will look up to the leaders for any big moves. They will respond according to their self-interests or perhaps some implicit understandings already agreed upon.

On the surface, it looks like there is a free flow of information in the stock market. The quantity of information available is huge and ever increasing. However, there is no free flow of the most relevant information to the small investors. When there is, it is usually after the facts. An examination of the information flow has been given in Chapter 2.

REASONS FOR A CRASH

We now proceed to explore why a market crash occurs. There are two kinds of market crashes: genuine and fake. A genuine crash signifies either the end of the world or the collapse of the capitalist system. Some examples are as follows: enemy nuclear missiles hitting New York and other American cities, a very massive natural disaster paralyzing the industrialized countries, a collapse of the world banking system triggering economic depression and chaos, and the Third-World oil producers declaring total war on the West. Any of the above examples will spell the death of the stock market. The other kind of crash is much less severe. It is temporary and recoverable by design. It is the fake crash that we are going to examine.

A genuine crash results directly from a great calamity beyond the control of the stock market. A fake crash should not be taken as a result of any external event. It is the direct consequence of some big players wanting to dump large quantities of stocks. The external events are only environmental factors supporting their actions. Two examples are the big crash of October 1987, and the prolonged crash of the Persian Gulf Crisis during the autumn of 1990. It is so easy for people to accept an external event as a true reason for a fake crash, thereby ignoring the real intentions behind the fake crash.

A major fund with big holdings can precipitate a crash on any day if it starts to liquidate its core portfolio. This will generate a chain reaction of panic sell bringing in the other funds and the small investors. Why should a major fund do that? The reasons are the same as in any other business: survival, growth and renewal. The opportunity for renewal is excellent in the stock trading business. When the market goes out of control, the big funds just need to dump their stocks, drive down prices, and start all over again from a low price level. No other business has this great potential for self-directed renewal.

There are three basic environmental conditions that lead to a fake crash: overheat, lack of cash, and uncertainty. Overheat and uncertainty will eventually lead to lack of cash, but not the other way round. Overheat is brought about by a number of factors. The most important of all is interest rate reduction which increases the money in circulation. Lower interest rates also discourage savings put into banks. As more money flows to the stock market, stock prices rise across the board. More investors will be drawn in and the bets go higher and higher. This kind of frenzy can easily feed on itself. Other factors can add to the intensity such as low inflation rate and economic expansion. Let us recall the previous diagram about a big mutual fund's core portfolio:

```
_____   Cyclical high record broken
Market price range  moving up due to overheat
_____   Cyclical low moving up
Market buffer widening
_____   Core-holding high $30  ----------------------
                                                    Fund's majority
                                                    holding is within
                                                    this price spread
Original cost of stock
_____   Core-holding low $5   ----------------------
```

In the above diagram, due to overheat of the market, the stock has risen to a higher cyclical range, thereby widening the market buffer without any price boost by the big fund. The fund is now in a better position than before. However, the fund manager is not a naive person to believe that this can last long.

First of all, it is now getting more and more expensive to trade on a daily basis because stock prices are going up steadily across the board. As the days go by, lesser quantities of stocks can be purchased due to higher prices. This means a larger price increase has to materialize to earn the same profit as before. Second, there is the temptation to sell the stocks now while prices are high and the market is hot. Third, the big fund finds that it is slowly losing control of the market. It is accustomed to see the market prices move according to its buy and sell activities. Now, the prices only move upward. After it sells a large quantity today, to continue trading, it has to buy the same quantity at a higher price tomorrow, thereby increasing its cost and risk.

If the overheat situation continues, all the cash available will be depleted. In other words, the big players are gradually being priced out of the market. This has got to end. The big fund is forced to initiate a correction and regain control of the market by flexing its muscles. The greatest leverage it has is the large core holdings of well-established companies. It is a complex decision about when, how, how much and how fast to dump the core holdings. Whichever means being adopted, the objective is to achieve the following: to reap as much profit as possible; to replenish the core stocks at lower prices; to drive down the cyclical range so that it will be cheaper to play again on a daily basis; and last but not least, to set the right stage for a future rally.

The second environmental condition, lack of cash, may be a result of overheat just described, or uncertainty about the future which poisons the investment climate. In other situations, lack of cash is the direct consequence of an increase in interest rates which takes money away from the stock market. It is also a direct consequence of security exchange regulations to reduce the margin rate allowed for

stocks. Faced with a sudden contraction of the money supply, the fund managers must reduce commitments in stocks
by cashing out, leading to a price drop across the board.

The consequence of lack of cash hinges on the width of
the market buffer. Further reduction of the market buffer
will trigger a dump from the core portfolio. For a big fund
manager, the thinning of the market buffer presents a
nightmare. When the core portfolio is subject to increasing
risks, it is better to initiate a sell to reap some profit first
and to replenish later at a lower price. A crash may appear
to the small investors as the most dreadful thing. For a big
fund manager, it is a logical solution for renewal of the
stock market.

The third environmental condition, uncertainty, refers
to all other kinds of external events, big or small.
Significant ones include the Persian Gulf Crisis, health
care reforms initiated by the Clinton Administration, death
of the Cold War, threats to brand names, price cutting by a
market leader, etc. Most of these uncertainties are limited
to one or few industries. When the uncertainty is localized,
chances for a general crash are reduced. The uncertainty
produces a mini or prolonged crash in the industries
affected, thereby releasing the cash which can possibly be
diverted to support the stocks of other industries.

The current bull market beginning in the winter of
1991 is full of mini crashes. It started with uncertainty in
the defense industry due to the breakup of the Soviet
Union. Then IBM began to slide under a cloud surrounding

the future of the mainframe computer. Next came the investigation and criticism by the Clinton Administration which battered the drug and health care industries. Before this was over, the brand names came under attack as Philip Morris announced price cutting of its famous cigarette brands. In early June 1993, even the fast-growing computer network industry was clobbered as 3Com lost almost 30% of its value in just one day on news of lower expected sales, followed by SynOptics on news of reduced prices for its products. Cisco and Novell also came under downward pressure. All of the above reactions reflect the nervousness of the market. Who knows which industry will be hit next?

Significant external events are always happening from time to time. How the stock market will react depends on how much the big funds want to capitalize on those events. Since the market has reacted strongly to these events in succession, the following are possible for the remainder of 1993 and beyond.

First, the current bull market beginning in late 1991 may be approaching the end. This will become a certainty when the inflation rate continues to increase, forcing the Federal Reserve to raise interest rates. When interest rates rise, less cash will flow to the stock maket. The fund managers will have to reduce commitments in stocks accordingly. This will lead to falling stock prices across the board. If this occurs gradually, a bear market will take hold and will last until there are good reasons for the bulls to come back.

Second, the current bull market may continue to adjust itself with localized crashes enabling money to move from one industry to another. This will occur if the inflation rate remains low in the presence of high unemployment and excess capacity in the factories. As of mid-1993, the US economy is only recovering slowly. The other industrialized countries are not out of a recession yet. Although the current bull market has traveled through a bumpy road, it should have a long way to go to take full advantage of the extended recovery until the world economy is in full bloom. Perhaps the institutions think that a mini crash here and there is the best way to keep the bulls around for a longer time.

Third, the current slow economic recovery is likely to extend over many more months. The big funds may find it difficult to keep the bulls around for too long. While stock prices are still high, it may be wise to force a general crash now to reap the profits and start the renewal process. A general crash will send a strong message about the displeasure of the financial markets regarding the pace of the economic recovery or about government policies to stimulate the economy.

Should a general crash occur in the latter half of 1993 or early 1994, the stock market would have a good chance for a quick rally several weeks later. The reason is that a stock market rally always depends on low interest rates and economic expansion, under which the profitability of public companies can improve. As of mid-1993, the world economy is expanding at a slow pace. The interest rates are still low compared with the previous few years, although some signs of renewed inflation begin to appear. This kind of environment will be able to nurture a rally after a general crash has occurred.

4 HOW TO PICK THE RIGHT STOCKS

The number of public companies in the United States stands at 5,000 and growing. You are bombarded daily with information about good and bad companies. You see stock price movements which often contradict with what you expect. Which stocks should you pick? It is really a tough decision to make.

You may spend days researching a company and its products. What are the most relevant data that can reasonably predict stock price movements? Where are the traps that may lead you to the wrong decisions? The hard fact remains that a stock cannot fly without institutional sponsorship. This chapter will identify and explain the crucial factors which account for institutional sponsorship. Once you begin to appreciate these fundamental factors, everything else will fall nicely into place.

WHICH STOCKS ARE CHEAP?

Before you buy something, it is natural to ask about the price and compare it with other similar products. You should not do this with stocks. The price of a product sold reflects its cost, plus a profit margin resulting from supply and demand. If the demand is weak and the supplier is desperate to sell, the profit margin may be less than zero, thus making it a loss to sell the product.

The price of a stock has a very small cost component equal to the cost of the paper, plus the entitlement to some dividends. The profit margin depends on the future of the company, which appears differently to different people. When an institutional investor likes the company, it buys the stock in big quantities, then the price goes up fast. The rest of the crowd sees this and joins in. Then the price goes up more and more. The reverse is also true.

When you invest in stocks, you must know exactly what your objective should be. Unlike a car or a dress, you buy a stock not for the purpose of enjoyment, utility, or pride of ownership. You buy a stock in order to sell it at a higher price. You must not become sentimental about a given industry, company or product. If a stock is going up, the price should not prevent you from owning it. The price only determines how many shares you can afford initially. You may wind up owning more when the stock splits. The broker's commission may add a little complexity to the consideration. Suppose you can only afford 50 shares at $100 per share. If the commissions for buy and sell total $100, you can only break even when the price goes to $102. Therefore you should expect the price to go beyond that point when you buy. In any case, you should not worry too much about the commission, because if the stock goes up and up, the commission will become an increasingly small percentage of your profit.

When a stock is falling, you should never believe that it is getting cheaper now to own. It may give you a nightmare. A falling stock means more people are selling than buying. You will never know the bottom until it stops falling for quite a while. A stock is cheapest when the big investors decide to support it at its lowest price level. This is where they accumulate as much as they can for leverage and profit taking later on. Because you do not know what the big investors plan to do, trying to guess the bottom is a risky business. It is better to wait until you can see a sustainable upturn.

The book value tends to give you a false impression of the value of a stock. The institutions seldom use the book value to determine a price to support. Why should they follow an accounting figure when they can get the lowest price in the marketplace? If a failed company goes to liquidation, the holders of its common stock will be the last group of creditors to get compensation. Therefore, they may wind up with nothing after liquidation.

Among other things, the book value includes machinery and inventory evaluated on cost basis at a time well before the liquidation. When trouble begins in a company, inventory usually piles up as a result of poor sales. The book value published at that time will give you an inflated figure.

When a company fails, its products are usually unattractive to the customers, and its machinery is inefficient. At liquidation time, all the assets are sold by auction, not on cost basis. How much will the assets be worth? If the inventory consists of raw materials like oil or timber, it will retain most of its values. If they are finished products such as out-of-fashion dresses or out-of-date computer parts, you probably have to pay the cost for hauling the inventory to the trash dump.

The P/E ratio is more meaningful especially when you compare it with other stocks. The P/E ratio is defined as the current stock price divided by the latest twelve-month earnings. Earnings will be discussed later in this chapter. It is commonly believed that the higher the ratio, the more expensive the stock appears. For those companies not making a profit, that is showing negative earnings, the P/E ratio has no meaning at all. Please see Table 4-1 for illustration.

Table 4-1: P/E Ratios of Major Companies in Selected Industries

Companies	P/E	Industries
Philip Morris	12	Cigarettes, food, brewery
Johnson & Johnson	18	Health care products
Merk	19	Drugs
Amgen	32	Biotech
Chrysler	27	Automobiles
Citicorp	19	Banking
Hewlett-Packard	21	Electronic instruments
General Dynamics	5	Defense
Intel	22	Semiconductors
Compaq	20	Personal Computers
Novell	38	Personal computer network software
Cisco	55	Computer network products
Oracle	52	Database software
S&P 500 Index	23	(Obtained from Fortune Magazine)

Source: Standard & Poor's Stock Guide, February 1993 issue.

There is an average P/E ratio for the Standard & Poor 500 Index, which comprises 500 selected stocks. It currently stands at around 23. This is high by historical standard. Before the crash of October 1987, the figure was 20, then it fell below 12 in early 1989 before making an upturn. So you can see in general how much stock prices relative to earnings have risen since then.

All kinds of interpretation can be drawn from the P/E ratios shown in Table 4-1. The P/E ratio of General Dynamics lags behind because of huge defense spending cuts. Due to their high P/E ratios, the companies currently favored by Wall Street are in the computer network and database software sectors, such as Novell, Cisco and Oracle. Because stock prices can change drastically in a short time, using the P/E ratio to interpret the performance of a stock can give a wrong impression. For instance, Leslie Fay, a manufacturer of women's apparel, had a good P/E of 5 in February 1993. The company went bankrupt a month later under a cloud of accounting irregularities. Suffice it to say that the higher the P/E ratio, the more expensive the stock will appear. This does not mean that the price cannot rise even higher, nor that there will soon be a correction.

Many small investors tend to use the price range of a stock in past years to determine whether the stock is expensive or not. This is merely a convenient way of doing things, but it poses a dangerous risk. A stock approaching last year's low may signify that the company is heading toward bankruptcy in a matter of months. It is cheap alright but it is useless. On the other hand, a good stock with growth momentum will successively break the previous year's high to reach unbelievable levels. It is expensive but it pays to own.

THE POWER OF FAITH

Everybody seems to take faith for granted. If you look around, you will find that the whole world works on just one fundamental principle, which is faith. You wake up in the morning to go to work. You never question your company may close down, leaving you with no office when you get there. On your way to work, you stop at the red light not because of the traffic law which you can ignore anytime. It is because you believe that other people will observe this rule, and that it will only take a while before your turn to go. At work, you do the best in your own specialized field without worrying that your colleagues may undo or mess up your work somewhere down the process. You receive your paycheck in U.S. dollars which you never question. Would you scream should your employer give you three times as much in Russian Rubles? You certainly would because the current state of the Russian economy is shaking your faith in the currency. Let us say if you do not have faith in the society, your work, and the people you come into contact with, you would probably be still lying in bed, wondering and worrying about what would happen next.

What does faith have to do with stocks? A lot! My grandmother is an old-fashioned woman. She does not understand stocks and never cares about the stock market. She had some savings and her best friend suggested she should buy some stocks. She was interested in only two companies which she knew had been around for quite a while: McDonald's and Coca-Cola. She bought 500 shares of Coke in 1986 and put away the stock certificates. Nobody in the family knew she had done that. When we were talking about the crash in October 1987, she asked which airline and how many people survived. Some time in February 1993, she mentioned that she owned some Coca-Cola shares. Coke was worth around $40 a share at that time. The stock has split three times: 3 for 1 in 1986, 2 for 1 in 1990, and 2 for 1 in 1992. The whole family was ecstatic and proud of her. Right now she is still pondering why those crazy stock certificates can bring in so much money.

There are several lessons to be learned from this case. First, it does not take expertise or research work to win big in the stock market. My grandmother relied solely on her faith in corporate America, her friend, and the stability of the consumer market in general. Second, she bought the stock of a well-established company in a traditional industry and held on for several years. This helped her survive the crash of 1987. Third, she only took one risk in the stock market since 1986. She might have lost all her savings if she took more risks, or might have multiplied her wealth many times.

EARNINGS: THE BOTTOM LINE

What can sustain the rise of a stock? There are thousands of indirect answers such as a growth company, good products, good management etc. The most relevant and direct answer is the profitability of the company which gives the big institutional investors a reason to buy and support the price. Basically, for a company to be profitable, it has to earn more money than all the costs it incurs. A company with increasing sales can be unprofitable if it fails to control its costs. Likewise, a lean and mean company does not require large sales increases to post impressive profits.

Profitability encompasses everything including sales volume, price, product quality, cost control, management strategy, competitive environment, governmental impacts, and so on. It is the final result of a company's performance in the marketplace. To put it simply, if you want to pick a good stock, look for companies which have a good profit record, or a good promise of upcoming profits.

The formula that Wall Street uses for measuring profitability is earnings. It is defined as net profit divided by the number of outstanding shares. Net profit is equal to total income minus total operating costs minus taxes. Earnings are reported by public companies on a quarterly and yearly basis. Net profit shows the financial result of everything that the company does in a competitive market environment.

The earnings formula is a simple and effective measure of company performance. Although the big investors can influence the price in either direction they please, they cannot ignore the bottom line, which is earnings. They can no longer support the stock price if a company fails to produce acceptable earnings results.

Although earning is the fundamental pillar for the stock price, all kinds of market condition can cause the price to move. If a company has good earnings prospects, its stock price will rebound even though there are temporary setbacks due to general market downturns. Nearly all investors understand the earnings formula, but not many pay enough attention to it. During conversations about stocks, earnings are only mentioned in passing. The topics usually cover products, industries, price wars, government regulations and so on, which may cancel each other out and do not affect earnings at all. The following diagram illustrates this point:

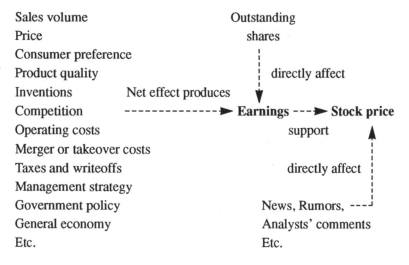

Since the stock market deals with the future. It is the expected earnings of a company that count. Secondly, absolute earnings do not correlate with the stock price. It is the change in earnings that determine the direction of the price. Thirdly, although earnings represent the bottom line, there is no reason that the stock price should automatically follow the earnings pattern. The big institutions sometimes like to interpret the earnings results as an excuse to influence the price.

Having pinned down this most crucial factor, small investors should now pay most attention to the earnings pattern over several quarters, and try to correlate them with the stock price. You will find that most stocks with steadily rising prices have steadily rising earnings to back them up.

SHARES OUTSTANDING

The number of outstanding shares can lift or weigh down the earnings, hence the stock price. The simple reason is demand and supply. When there are too many shares out there for people to buy (dilution is the technical term), how much can the stock price go up? If a company wants to benefit the investors, the best way is to buy back some of its own shares in the open market. In this way, the earnings figure will improve on the balance sheet, and the number of shares actually issued will be reduced.

If a company issues more and more shares without increasing profits to back it up, the stock price will become too heavy to fly. The splitting of shares usually occurs when the stock price of a company has reached a high point where it is considered too expensive for investors. The first couple of splits normally benefit the stockholders, because the remaining growth momentum of the company can carry the price once again up to its previous high levels. When this momentum begins to fade, the large quantity of shares tends to weigh down the stock price. Novell provides a good example. The stock splits in 1990 and 1991 saw the price continue its upward trend to pre-split levels in a few months. However, the split that occurred in 1992 found the price rather sticky around $30 for many months.

The number of outstanding shares also accounts for the magnitude of the price rise. When the company performs well, there will be more buyers chasing after the company's shares. The smaller the quantity of shares issued, the higher the stock price will be bid up. The potential of future stock splits also depends heavily on the present number of outstanding shares. Before the decision on a split, the directors of the company must have consulted with the institutional investors with large holdings of the company's shares. An understanding must have been reached to safeguard or promote the values of their present holdings. If the number of outstanding shares is already too large, there will be resistance against a split because it will be difficult to support the price of too large a quantity. Table 4-2 illustrates this relationship.

Table 4-2: Outstanding Common Shares, Price Range and Stock Splits

Company	Outstanding Common Shares March 93 (Mn)	1992 Price Range Low	High	Years When Stock Split Since 1989
SynOptics	19.5	18 3/4	95 1/2	1990
Cisco	60.9	32 1/4	80 3/4	1991, 92
Cabletron	28.2	42 1/8	85 1/4	
Novell	300.6	22 1/2	33 1/2	1990, 91,92
Microsoft	275.1	65 3/4	95	1990, 91, 92
Borland	26.2	19 3/4	86 3/4	
Oracle	142.0	12	28 5/8	1989
Informix	24.2	6 5/8	37 3/4	1992
Sybase	22.0	20 1/2	49 3/4	
Intel	208.2	46 1/2	91 1/2	
General Dynamics	29.7	53 3/8	107 7/8	
Boeing	339.3	33 1/8	54 5/8	1989, 90
Coca Cola	1310.0	35 5/8	45 3/8	1990, 92
Fruit of the Loom	75.1	26 1/2	49 5/8	
Chrysler	341.9	11 1/2	33 7/8	
Ford	488.1	27 3/4	48 7/8	
Merck	1147.0	40 1/2	56 5/8	1992
Johnson & Johnson	654.7	43	58 3/4	1989, 92
Amgen	135.2	49 1/4	78 1/8	1990, 91
Synergen	24.8	31 3/4	75	1991
Capital Cities/ABC	16.4	410 1/8	521	

Source: Standard & Poor's Stock Guide, March 1993 Issue.

As Table 4-2 shows, a smaller share number is usually associated with a bigger rise in the stock price. The companies with relatively small numbers of shares include: SynOptics, Cabletron, Borland, Informix, Sybase, General Dynamics, and Synergen. On the other hand, with over 1.3 billion shares outstanding, no wonder Coca-Cola has to install a plan to consistently buy back some of its shares in order to support the price.

The absolute number of shares cannot be viewed in a vacuum. It must be seen in the light of the company's sales and profits. If the number of outstanding shares is small and the sales and profits of the company are fast increasing, chances for further price increases and stock splits will be very high. Finally, Table 4-2 shows the high price of Capital Cities/ABC. This company had sales of $5.4 billion in 1992 while the number of shares outstanding was only 16.4 million. This should speak volumes for the relationship between share prices and shares issued.

BIG COMPANIES OR SMALL COMPANIES?

Every industry has good-performing companies or otherwise. Although the companies within a given industry compete among themselves, the rise of the stock price of one does not necessarily mean the fall of another. More often than not, the good performance of one company, especially a leader, tends to pull up the rest of the industry. The poor performance of a company also tends to drag down the rest. There are some exceptions related to very specific cases. The legal battle between Intel and AMD regarding the copyright of the 386 and 486 chips saw the share prices of the combatants moving in opposite directions when the judge handed down the decisions.

Before you buy a stock, you should have some idea about the size of the company and where it stands in its own industrial sector. A big company or an industrial leader presents many advantages to investors. First of all, a big company has significant institutional sponsorship. When the stock price of a big company comes down, the descend tends to be less violent. Thus the small investors have enough time to cash out. The same is true when the price goes up. A big company normally has a lot of shares outstanding. So it takes a much larger amount of money to buy up the price. It also takes quite some time for the price to ascend. The small investors have plenty of time to observe the trend before going in.

The stock price of a big company normally moves in line with the general economy. Many people may not know about a particular industry, but most people can get a good grasp of the current economic situation through daily conversations or just reading the news headlines. At the bottom of the last recession around mid 1991, the stocks of most big companies were flat around their lows. If you have picked just a couple of them, you will have seen a good return on your investments by early 1993.

To improve its earnings hence the stock price, a big company can do many things. It can sell some of its assets such as land to raise cash for immediate needs. It can obtain or renegotiate a bank loan rather easily. It can sell an unprofitable division which will result in lowering its operating expenses and reducing its long-term debt. A big company can reorganize and trim its work force thereby saving millions of dollars. In special cases such as a merger, a big company may have spent over 100 million dollars in one year. This large sum is a one time charge only. The absence of this charge in the account for the following year will automatically boost its earnings. Finally, the effect of a tax writeoff due to a heavy loss in the previous year cannot be ignored. It should be noted that none of the above requires raising revenues which depend heavily on external market conditions beyond the company's control.

During bad times when a big company is having trouble, institutional investors seldom make an exodus. They rather prefer to see how the company cuts its costs and manages a turnaround. If the big company succeeds in doing that, the earnings will already have improved significantly. By the time the economy picks up, increased revenues will propel the stock price to a high level. Chrysler is a good example during the period between mid-1991 and early 1993. Therefore, you should never underestimate the skyrocketing effect of a big company turnaround.

Small companies have little cash to cushion the impacts of bad times. They do not have enough fat in their organizations to trim. Institutional investors tend to exit en masse when revenues cannot keep pace. That is why the stock prices for small companies come down really fast and may fall through the bottom when there are bad news about revenues. A small company depends very heavily on one thing: sustained revenue growth to back up its stock price. The risks therefore are greater. However, all companies, big or small, have to go through this stage one time or another. The point is how to avoid picking the wrong ones. The more relevant point should be how to pick the same ones as the institutions do.

The direct approach to investigate small companies is to observe the market reaction before you go in. The relevant facts are as follows. The number of institutions and their total percentage holdings in the small company in question should be significant and consistent. Good revenue growth should accompany earnings growth for a few consecutive quarters. The stock price should have been rising accordingly. The trade volumes on rising days should be significantly greater than those on falling days. Better still, the stock has been able to break previous highs again and again.

After you have verified all the above, you can go in with confidence that you have picked the right stock. After all, why take the unnecessary risk of second-guessing the stock performance of a small company? Take some time to check out the institutional sponsorship, and allow the company time to prove itself in the market. You should not worry about missing the boat. If you have picked a good performer, the stock price will go up and up, followed by stock splits, maybe a takeover. The bonanza will come later, not at the initial stages of growth.

WHICH INDUSTRIES ARE BEST?

Most people have their own favorite industries. The reasons vary. You may be fascinated by the aerospace industry. Your good friend may be a pharmacist so you are interested in the pharmaceutical industry. You may be a computer programmer so you think you know more about the computer industry. There are glamorous and growth industries which people like, and traditional industries which people tend to ignore. In any case, you buy a stock in order to sell it later for a profit. You do not buy a stock for the pride of ownership. Industry or company favorites should play no part in your investment decisions. There- fore, you should analyze things objectively, and go into the best stocks regardless of industry and company.

At the beginning of a bull market, the stock prices of all major companies rise due to the large amount of cash inflow. After several months when the inflow has stabilized, the money will start cycling from one industry to another. If you have only one industry favorite, you will have to wait for the next cycle to hit. It is always better to know about the other industries and go after the money flow.

The following is a survey of various industries. The purposes are to point out the different characteristics between them, and to highlight the important factors to be considered for investment. Within each industry, a statistical table will show the performance of major companies. The statistics will be out of date by the time this book hits the bookstore, but it should not matter since the objective is to illustrate a point rather than dwelling on the figures per se. The readers should not construe that the companies selected are recommended for investment. Those companies are selected to substantiate or convey a point. The readers may want to pick up any of those companies and use the methods recommended in this book for their own further investigation.

First, take the traditional **consumer industries** like food, beverage, and tobacco. The giant companies in this industry have made tremendous profits during the 1980s. If you have invested in McDonald, Philip Morris, Pepsico, or Coca-Cola back in the mid-1980s, you will have walked away with several times your original investment. Besides rising stock prices, the stocks of these companies have split at least once since then. The same can be said about other consumer industries like soap, body care items, apparels, and toys.

The long-term prospects for the traditional consumer industries look really good. The American consumer market has grown dramatically for the past two decades. Some experts think that it has matured. However, we are only seeing the tip of the iceberg overseas. The future belongs to those companies which are able to exploit the expanding consumer markets of the globe.

The world population shows no signs of declining despite wars, plagues and natural disasters. The main thrust of the population increase comes from Asia, South America and Africa. More importantly, the most populous countries of Asia like China, India, Indonesia and many others are going through a period of rapid economic growth with tremendous opportunities for consumer products never seen before. The countries in South America seem to have sorted out their problems, and are on the verge of sustained economic growth. The countries of Africa are patiently waiting for their turn. Do not forget the large populations of Russia and Eastern Europe who will add to the huge consumer demands already existing.

The giant American companies of consumer products are in an excellent position to profit from the fast-expanding world markets since they have long established their brand names overseas plus an extensive worldwide sales network. Furthermore, they have been tapping into the cheap labor force for decades by establishing factories overseas to manufacture their products under license. If you buy into these companies, it looks like the world population will stand on your side. In this connection, investing in funeral companies may not be a bad idea. You may laugh at it, but who can resist the call from Heaven? The only handicap is that funeral companies are not known to operate on a worldwide basis thus unable to exploit the potential of world population and economic growth.

The traditional consumer industry is easy to enter, such as the restaurant business. Therefore competition is fierce, reducing the profit margin. You have to find those companies which can successfully fight off the competition by developing a so-called niche market that distinguishes themselves from others.

Coke and Pepsi are good examples. They have separately cultivated their own special groups of consumers. People seem to like the name as much as the carbonated sweet water. In addition, Coke and Pepsi have been able to cut across cultural and racial boundaries. In this respect, you may notice the extraordinary success of Walt Disney in the entertainment field. This company has proved its exceptional ability to market American culture in other countries with its theme parks, movies, and animated characters. It has created such a high degree of product differentiation that its business almost becomes a monopoly.

One uncertainty surfacing lately in the consumer industry is about brand-name products impacted by generic brands. In early April 1993, Philip Morris announced that it would cut prices of its famous cigarette brands to counter the generic onslaught. In one day the stock lost 20% of its value. This is followed by downward pressures on nearly all companies selling brand-name products. Whether this is over-reaction remains to be seen. A brand name takes a lot of money and effort to cultivate. It becomes more or less a habit or tradition after gradual implantation into the consumer psyche. Hence if it dies at all, it will be a slow death. You have to see how much impact the generic brands can exert on the profitability of brand-name products before you can pronounce the death of brand names.

The consumer industry is the biggest comprising many companies with multi-billion-dollar sales. A diversity of companies can be grouped under this industry which covers food, beverages, clothing, soap and other body-care items, toys, wholesale, retail, leisure, entertainment, broadcasting and publishing.

Table 4-3 shows the performance of selected major companies during the period between 1992 and 1993. In general, most stock prices have fallen due to weakness in consumer demands. So companies continue to restructure and cut employment, as consumer demands cannot expect to pick up significantly. However, most big companies are making profits already mainly due to cost cutting efforts. The improvement in the profit picture has led to a general increase in institutional commitments as shown by their percentage holdings.

You will notice the huge loss incurred by Sears which strangely enough, has produced a higher stock price and more institutional holdings. The reason is that Sears is divesting its holdings in Allstate Insurance and Dean Witter, which is expected to improve its profitability. The number of shares issued by Sears is really small relative to the size of the company. So are the shares of Philip Morris, Kmart, ConAgra, Fleming, and many others.

Table 4-3. Leading Companies in Consumer Goods & Services

Company Ranking by 1992 Sales	Profits 1992 ($Mn)	Out- standing Shares (Mn)	Share Prices ($) 1992 High	Apr 93 High	Institution Holdings (%) 1992	1993
Sears Roebuck	-3932	346	48	55	58	62
Wal-Mart Stores	+1995	2298	33	32 1/4	29	30
Philip Morris	+ 552	340	54 5/8	38 3/8	47	44
K mart	+ 941	407	28 1/8	23 7/8	77	73
Procter&Gamble	+1872	681	55 3/4	50 3/8	44	47
PepsiCo	+ 374	796	43 3/8	43 1/8	56	58
ConAgra	+ 372	247	35 3/4	27 1/2	36	35
RJR Nabisco	+ 299	1160	11 3/4	9 1/8	11	24
Johnson&Johnson	+1030	655	58 3/4	43 7/8	52	59
Sara Lee	+ 761	484	32 1/2	28 1/8	45	48
Coca-Cola	+1664	1307	45 3/8	43 1/8	54	52
Time Warner	+ 86	372	29 3/4	35 1/8	37	72
Fleming	+ 113	37	35 1/8	32 7/8	75	83
Anheuser-Busch	+ 918	277	60 3/4	53 3/4	55	56
Marriott	+ 85	101	21 7/8	26 1/2	35	46
Waste Mangmt.	+ 850	489	46 5/8	34	50	53
Walt Disney	+ 817	524	45 1/4	45 1/8	40	43
Colgate-Palmol.	+ 477	160	60 5/8	66 3/8	48	62
Paramount Comm.	+ 261	118	48 3/4	52 5/8	48	53
R.R.Donnelley	+ 235	159	33 3/4	29 5/8	67	72
Times Mirror	- 67	129	38 3/8	33 1/2	45	45
Avon Products	+ 175	72	60 1/4	62 3/8	68	79
Nike	+ 329	76	90 1/4'	76 5/8	53	51
Reebok	+ 115	89	35 5/8	36 7/8	53	68
Hasbro	+ 179	87	35 7/8	33 1/4	70	72
Mattel	+ 144	96	27	24 3/4	66	84
Fruit of the Loom	+ 179	75	49 5/8	43 1/2	64	79
Gerber Products	+ 128	73	38 1/2	30 7/8	56	53

Sources: Fortune Magazine, Standard & Poor's Stock Guide

The **high-tech** industry is characterized by growth and competition. Hence it has high potential and high risk. A high-tech product emphasizes on performance and cost. Technology advancement delivers more performance and drives down costs. A company losing the technological edge cannot survive. The products get obsolete quickly, so are the machinery for making those products. Capital expenses are high due to initial research outlays and constant updates required. Because of the availability of venture capital, entry into the high-tech industry is not very difficult, thus intensifying the competition.

Price cutting is commonplace which drives many companies out of business. The personal computer price war initiated by Compaq Computer in 1992 illustrates the carnage. Well-established companies cannot stay complacent. Look at what has happened to IBM, Digital, and Wang Laboratories during 1992. Unlike traditional-industry giants protected by brand names, high-tech giants can lose their market shares easily to small upstarts which are much more adaptable to fast changing market conditions. Adding to the fast pace and high competition is the copyright contention between companies. The legal battles between Intel and AMD are well known to investors.

The stock prices certainly reflect the volatility of this industry. Small high-tech companies come and go. Quite a few made impressive growth such as Novell, Cisco and SynOptics which represent the leaders of the emerging computer network sector. The growth of software companies is also phenomenal, exemplified by Microsoft, Oracle,

Lotus and Borland. The wireless telecommunications sector seems to be exploding with the widespread use of cellular phones where Motorola is the leading supplier.

The next wave on the horizon looks like the multimedia sector, which attempts to integrate the functions of the personal computer, the television, the telephone, and the stereo set to form a complete system. It is not clear what the consumers really want at this stage. It will be interesting to see what kinds of multimedia product will come up and capture the consumer demands.

For investment in high-tech companies, it is advisable to limit your view to the medium term. Many high-tech products have short life cycles less than a year. The stock price varies with their introduction and obsolescence unless the company pulls through with another successful product.

Table 4-4 shows the performance of the high-tech industry for the period between 1992 and 1993. The biggest casualty befell the manufacturers of mainframe computers as evidenced by IBM and Amdahl. The profit picture is mixed where some companies like IBM, Digital Equipment, Westinghouse and Xerox incurred heavy losses. Whereas others like General Electric, Eastman Kodak, Intel and Microsoft reaped great profits. You will notice that this industry exhibits the biggest fluctuations in profits, share prices and institutional holdings due to the nature of the products and the intensely competitive environment.

Table 4-4. Leading Companies in High-Tech Industry.

Company Ranking by 1992 Sales	Profits 1992 ($Mn)	Out-standing Shares (Mn)	Share Prices ($) 1992 High	Apr 93 High	Institution Holdings (%) 1992	1993
IBM	- 4965	572	100 3/8	53 1/8	49	41
Gen. Electric	+ 4725	854	87 1/2	96	52	54
Eastman Kodak	+ 1146	326	50 3/4	56 3/8	52	59
Xerox	- 1020	95	82 1/4	83 1/2	77	84
Hewlett-Pack.	+ 549	251	85	76 1/2	50	55
Digital Equip.	- 2796	132	65 1/2	44 3/4	68	64
Motorola	+ 453	270	53 1/4	74 7/8	71	80
Westinghouse	- 1291	346	21 1/8	15 7/8	48	41
Rockwell Intl.	- 1036	219	29 3/8	34 7/8	51	53
Raytheon	+ 635	136	53 1/2	59 3/8	69	74
Unisys	+ 361	162	11 3/4	13 3/4	21	29
Texas Instr.	+ 247	83	52 1/4	59 1/2	67	76
Apple	+ 530	118	70	52 1/2	69	65
Honeywell	+ 247	137	38	35 1/8	72	71
Intel	+ 1067	209	91 1/2	121	73	80
Compaq	+ 213	78	49 3/8	53 3/8	50	62
Sun Micro.	+ 173	105	36 1/8	30 5/8	62	80
Seagate Tech.	+ 63	67	22 3/8	16 1/4	48	71
Microsoft	+ 708	280	95	94 3/4	29	34
Amdahl	- 7	113	20 5/8	6 1/2	45	38
Polaroid	+ 99	47	35	34 1/8	77	76
Computer Sci.	+ 68	17	84	80 1/2	72	76
Tandem	- 41	112	15 7/8	12 3/8	68	71
Aut.Data Proc.	+ 256	142	55 5/8	52 7/8	68	71
Wang Lab.	- 357	171	7 1/2	5/8	25	19
National Semi.	- 120	107	14 1/8	14	54	73
AMD	+ 245	88	21 1/2	32 7/8	43	56
Storage Tech.	+ 16	41	78	28 5/8	84	51
Computer Assoc.	+ 163	168	20 3/4	24 3/8	48	52

Sources: Fortune Magazine, Standard & Poor's Stock Guide

The **aerospace** industry is clouded by uncertainties due to the collapse of the Soviet Union and the end of the Cold War. As the U.S. Government scales down defense spendings, revenues flowing to defense contractors have been shrinking. The future success of defense companies rests on the speed of conversion of their technological prowess from military to commercial applications.

Boeing is one company that does not depend on military contracts as much as the others because of its huge commercial aircraft business in the world market. However, the company is losing market shares in recent years to Airbus from Europe while other American aircraft manufacturers do not appear to be serious competitors. In the short term, the way to survive for all defense companies is to trim fat and cut costs.

As an interesting exception, General Dynamics prefers to sell some of its divisions to provide better returns for the stockholders. After the sales, long-term debt was greatly reduced. The earnings picture improved dramatically from a loss of $14 per share in 1990, to a gain of $12 in 1991, and further on to $22 in 1992. As a result, the stock price doubled to over $110 in February 1993. Hence you see that a company can benefit the stockholders even in the declining defense industry by simply selling its assets.

Although most leading companies in this industry have suffered losses in 1992, the stock prices have not seen major declines. On the other hand, institutional holdings generally increased from 1992 to 1993. One explanation lies in the relatively small numbers of shares issued by these companies. The other explanation is the high-tech potential of defense companies which represents a big asset to be sold for cash, or exploited for commercial use. Table 4-5 shows the performance of the leading companies in the aerospace industry.

Table 4-5. Leading Companies in Aerospace Industry

Company Ranking by 1992 Sales	Profits 1992 ($Mn)	Out- standing Shares (Mn)	Share Prices ($) 1992 High	Apr 93 High	Institution Holdings (%) 1992	1993
Boeing	+552	340	54 5/8	38 3/8	47	44
United Tech.	-287	124	57 7/8	50 1/2	69	77
McDonnell Doug.	-781	39	78	63 1/4	36	41
Allied-Signal	-712	142	62	70 1/2	56	68
Lockheed	-283	61	58 3/8	65	62	94
General Dyn.	+815	31	107 7/8	99 3/4	51	54
Textron	-355	88	44 7/8	49 5/8	61	66
Martin Marietta	+345	47	70 1/2	75 1/8	64	80
Northrop	+121	47	34 7/8	39 3/8	43	61
Grumman	-123	34	25	38 1/4	34	37

Sources: Fortune Magazine, Standard & Poor's Stock Guide

The **banking and finance** industry is most sensitive to interest rate changes. When the Federal Reserve lowers the interest rates, the banks will pay less to borrow money, thus increasing their profit margins. Lower interest rates bring about a wave of consumer refinancing of real estate and other long-term debts. This generates huge revenues for financial institutions. Lower interest rates stimulate the real estate market and usually result in higher real estate prices. Because real estates are used to back up the loans, higher prices mean higher asset values for financial institutions. All of the above combine to give stock prices a strong push.

Table 4-6 shows that it has been a banner year for the banking and finance industry between 1992 and 1993. Nearly all major companies made decent profits, and the stock prices advanced accordingly. Student Loan Marketing is perhaps the only exception where the stock price has come down. This is due to possible policy changes by the Clinton Administration to provide for direct government financing of student loans.

Table 4-6. Leading Companies in Banking, Finance and Insurance.

Company Ranking by 1992 Sales	Profits 1992 ($Mn)	Out- standing Shares (Mn)	Share Prices ($)		Institution Holdings (%)	
			1992 High	Apr 93 High	1992	1993
Citicorp	+ 722	367	22 1/2	30 7/8	51	52
Fed.Natl.Mort.	+ 1623	273	77 1/4	83 3/4	81	86
BankAmerica	+ 1492	349	49 3/4	53 7/8	55	61
American Exp.	+ 461	478	25 3/8	29 3/4	62	69
Salomon	+ 550	110	39	39 1/4	60	63
Chemical Bank	+ 1086	247	39 1/2	44 1/8	42	73
NationsBank	+ 1145	253	53 3/8	57 7/8	n.a.	59
Merrill Lynch	+ 894	104	66 3/4	78	56	60
J.P. Morgan	+ 1382	192	70 1/2	74 3/8	73	68
Chase Manh.	+ 639	156	30 3/8	38	54	60
Aetna Life	+ 56	110	48 7/8	52 7/8	76	82
Morgan Stanley	+ 511	75	67 7/8	66 1/4	37	50
Bankers Trust	+ 761	83	70 1/8	78	75	77
Fed.Home Loan	+ 622	179	49 1/4	52	70	77
Banc One	+ 781	232	53 1/2	61 1/2	51	56
ITT	- 885	119	72 1/8	84 1/4	65	71
Travelers	- 658	142	27 5/8	30 1/4	67	76
Wells Fargo	+ 283	55	86 3/8	125	65	65
Student Loan	+ 394	89	76	49	81	91

Sources: Fortune Magazine, Standard & Poor's Stock Guide

The **automobile** industry is characterized by long product cycles lasting several years. The institutional investors seem to like this kind of stability thus providing steady sponsorship. General Motors has not been profitable since 1990, neither has Ford since 1991. Yet their stock prices fluctuate within relatively narrow margins. The rising star is Chrysler, whose turnaround propelled the stock price from a low of $11 in 1992 to over $40 in April 1993. The new products from Chrysler are currently well received by the consumers.

The automobile industry is highly competitive for a company failing to differentiate its products to make them stand out against the others. Since 1992, competition from Japan has subsided somewhat. It is not certain whether American companies have turned the tide. American automakers have let their quality image slip for over a decade. This cannot possibly be made up in a few years' time after consumer confidence has been eroded.

During the 1980s, riding high on their quality achievement, all major Japanese automakers have established manufacturing facilities on U.S. soil to circumvent possible import restrictions. They have successfully cultivated a new image for making high-performance deluxe automobiles to compete with the high-price European makes. The Lexus, Acura and Infiniti have received high praise and have cut into the European market shares. On the other hand, the American automakers have not responded vigorously to the challenge in the high-margin product lines, and seem to be content to stay on the sideline.

In the lower price range, Japanese cars have retreated to some extent due to price disadvantage resulting from a stronger Yen. The major automakers in Japan are going through the most difficult period in the early 1990s. They are not able to subsidize the prices of Japanese cars sold in the United States. As a result, the U.S. market has already seen a comparatively larger price increase for Japanese cars. This should present a good opportunity for American automakers to recapture some of the lost market shares.

Table 4-7 shows the huge losses of GM and Ford for 1992. However, this does not affect the stock prices much because the whole auto industry is rebounding gradually. The other reason is the small numbers of outstanding shares relative to the sizes of these two companies. The improvement of the auto industry also pushes up the stock prices of auto parts manufacturers such as Goodyear, TRW and Dana despite their losses in 1992. You will notice the low stock price of Navistar, the truck manufacturer. This reinforces the point that too many shares issued can weigh down a stock.

Table 4-7 also includes manufacturers of farm machinery and equipment. The major companies like Teneco, Caterpillar and Black & Decker all incurred losses for 1992. These companies have a significant export business which has been going through a slump in recent years.

Table 4-7. Leading Companies in Automobiles,
Machinery and Parts.

Company Ranking by 1992 Sales	Profits 1992 ($Mn)	Out-standing Shares (Mn)	Share Prices ($) 1992 High	Apr 93 High	Institution Holdings (%) 1992	1993
General Motor	-23498	707	44 3/8	42 5/8	38	40
Ford Motor	- 7385	490	48 7/8	55 7/8	52	56
Chrysler	+ 723	342	33 7/8	44	42	55
Tenneco	- 1323	169	46	49 1/8	48	48
Goodyear Tire	- 659	72	76 1/8	80 1/2	59	72
Caterpillar	- 2435	101	62 1/8	69 3/8	66	68
TRW	- 156	63	60 1/4	68 1/8	52	55
Deere	+ 37	76	54	60 7/8	76	81
Dana	- 382	46	48 1/4	49 1/2	63	72
Black&Decker	- 334	83	26 7/8	19 3/8	55	65
Navistar Intl.	- 212	254	4 1/8	3	44	39

Sources: Fortune Magazine, Standard & Poor's Stock Guide

The **transportation** industry is sensitive to the state of the general economy. As the economy expands, more goods are moving between factories, and from factories to consumers. More people are also traveling for business and leisure purposes.

The railroad stocks have picked up since the slow economic recovery beginning in early 1992. The railroad industry belongs to the past, but contrary to popular belief it is very solid. For many types of goods, especially automobiles, transportation by rail is most economical. In addition, railroad companies own a lot of land which is a non-depreciable hidden asset on the balance sheet. Institutions like to invest in this kind of traditional but solid industry.

The other land transportation industry comprises the trucking companies. They provide convenient door-to-door delivery, but are limited by the bulk of the goods to be carried. The trucking companies compete intensely with one another. Furthermore, they are subject to competition from small independent owner-operators.

Sea transportation also picks up when the economy expands. It depends heavily on exports and imports. When the global economy recovers completely resulting in more trade between nations, exports and imports will reach their peaks.

The U.S. domestic airline industry has been in a difficult situation since deregulation. Many things can exert a great impact on their operations, such as bad weather, the price of oil, world terrorism, defective airplane design, etc. Adding to these are the cut-throat competition, high capital cost, over-capacity, tight scheduling pressure, and labor problems. The consolation is that it is a glamorous industry supported by an ever-expanding travel market. The survival of an airline depends ultimately on management's ability to control costs while providing safe, reliable and pleasant services to the customers.

Table 4-8 shows the performance of the domestic airline industry where all the major airlines incurred heavy losses in 1992. One exception is the lean and mean Southwest Airlines whose stock price rose steadily in accordance with profits. At the same time, institutional investors were cashing out as evidenced by their reduced percentage holdings. You will notice that many companies in the transportation industry have issued relatively few shares especially for UAL and American President. That is why the stocks have managed to receive substantial institutional sponsorship which lends support to the high stock prices despite an unimpressive performance.

Table 4-8. Leading Companies in Transportation Industry.

Company Ranking by 1992 Sales	Profits 1992 ($Mn)	Out-standing Shares (Mn)	Share Prices ($) 1992 High	Apr 93 High	Institution Holdings (%) 1992	1993
AMR	- 935	75	80 1/4	71 5/8	84	83
UAL	- 957	24	159	149 3/4	74	77
Delta Airlines	- 506	49	75 1/4	60 1/4	64	67
CSX	+ 20	103	73 5/8	78 1/8	57	61
Fed. Express	- 114	54	56 1/8	56 3/8	70	79
US Air	-1229	47	18 3/8	24 3/4	66	60
Norfolk South.	+ 558	141	67 1/2	66 3/8	59	58
Burlington No.	+ 278	88	47 5/8	58 7/8	63	70
Consol. Freight.	- 81	35	19 5/8	18 3/4	69	69
Roadway Serv.	+ 147	39	77 3/4	65 1/2	62	66
Consol. Rail	+ 282	79	48 3/8	60 1/2	77	86
Am. President	+ 57	13	48	50 1/4	95	68
Santa Fe Pacific	- 105	181	14 1/8	16 3/8	29	68
Southwest Air.	+ 104	92	29 7/8	43	84	64

Sources: Fortune Magazine, Standard & Poor's Stock Guide

The **pharmaceutical** and **biotech** companies used to be the favorites of institutional investors for good reasons. American companies in this field are leading the world in both research and financial strength. The fear of competition is minimal because of patent protection. The market potential sees no limit because there will be more people in this world, more diseases to be discovered, and better cures to be invented. In biotechnology, tempering with genes can bring results which stretch the human imagination to its limits.

These two industries are almost recession-proof. Prices are cost plus, not subject to supply and demand. Despite heavy research outlays, all major companies like Johnson & Johnson, Bristol-Myers Squibb, Merck, and Amgen are reaping impressive profits. Based on Fortune Magazine, the profit to sale ratios in 1992 for Merck and Amgen are 20% and 32% respectively. This contrasts with other star performers like Intel (18%) and Chrysler (2%).

Besides good present earnings, the pharmaceutical and biotech stocks are supported by the potential earnings of approved patents and research work in the pipeline. Potential earnings of course are subject to interpretation and orchestration, but they are powerful tools for managing the stock price in either direction.

During the spring of 1991, the economy looked depressed. The stock market was mired in doldrums because there were no exciting news about good earnings. Most stocks had either fallen or stayed flat resulting in a lot of investment cash floating around. The biotech stocks suddenly took off and reached unbelievable heights within a matter of months. For instance, Amgen went from $19 to $63, Synergen from $10 to $64, and U.S. Bioscience from $17 to $45. The last two companies never made a profit since 1989. How can one explain this phenomenon if not for the availability of cash and the orchestration of potential profits? As expected, the high flying did not last long. The big investors who made this happen cashed out fast, leaving the enthusiastic followers burned.

In January 1993, the Clinton Administration took over. One of its priorities is health care reform. While the Administration was working on the reform plan, uncertainty was brewing about government price controls and tighter regulations. Then came government reports and criticisms about drug companies charging unfair prices. Under these circumstances, the pharmaceutical stocks took a series of beatings. When the reform plan is complete, legislative battles will ensue. How long this will take is indeterminable, so is the fate of the health care reform bill.

Under the pressure of health care reform, Merck and some other drug companies have volunteered to keep the prices down for some drugs. The price pressure will surely hurt the profits of drug companies. It is difficult to predict how low the big investors will allow the drug stocks to come down. It is also premature to say that drug and biotech stocks will lose the favoritism bestowed by big investors.

Table 4-9 underscores the cost-plus nature of the pharmaceutical and biotech industries as evidenced by the extraordinary profits earned in 1992. However, the stock prices have been slashed significantly due to possible government price control. Institutional holdings remain high. This means that the institutions sold part of their holdings at high prices and then replenished them at low prices. If the institutions do not desert this industry, the chance for a rebound is great. The question is when. Many major companies in this industry have split their shares during the early 1990s. If a rebound occurs, the large quantities of shares may prevent the stock prices reaching their previous high levels.

Table 4-9. Leading Companies in Pharmaceuticals and Biotech.

Company Ranking by 1992 Sales	Profits 1992 ($Mn)	Out- standing Shares (Mn)	Share Prices ($)		Institution Holdings (%)	
			1992 High	Apr 93 High	1992	1993
Johnson &Johnson	+1030	655	58 3/4	43 7/8	52	59
Bristol-Myers	+1962	518	90 1/8	62 3/8	50	53
Merck	+1984	1145	56 5/8	37 3/4	56	52
Abbott Lab.	+1239	835	34 1/4	28 3/8	51	51
Am.Home Prod.	+ 1461	313	84 1/4	67 3/4	61	62
Pfizer	+ 811	325	87	68 5/8	68	66
Eli Lilly	+ 709	293	87 3/4	49 3/8	65	71
Warner-Lambert	+ 644	135	79 1/4	74 1/4	63	69
Amer. Cyanamid	+ 395	90	66 3/8	53 1/4	62	64
Rhone-Poulenc R.	+ 438	138	69 3/8	48 5/8	21	21
Schering-Plough	+ 720	200	70 1/8	68 1/2	59	64
Upjohn	+ 324	175	45 7/8	30 3/4	49	57
Amgen	+ 358	135	78 1/4	41 3/4	64	67

Sources: Fortune Magazine, Standard & Poor's Stock Guide

The **health care** industry comprises private hospitals, health maintenance organizations (HMOs), medical technology and supplies manufacturers. The drug companies which have just been discussed also come under this industry.

The runaway health care cost in the United States is now approaching $1 trillion per year which is about 15% of the gross domestic product. Despite this huge expense, about 37 million Americans now go without health insurance, and the quality of health care does not appear to be improving. This sad situation has prompted the cry for drastic reforms.

Where does the health care money go? According to Fortune Magazine (5/17/93), 39% of total health care cost is absorbed by hospitals, 19% goes to physicians, 10% goes to dentists, and 9% goes to drugs and medical equipment. Where does the profit go? Bristol-Myers and Merck each reaped a profit close to $2 billion in 1992. The leading hospital enterprises like Humana and U.S. Healthcare earned $122 million and $200 million respectively in 1992. Doctors and dentists are known to be among the best-paid professionals.

The possible profit slashing effect brought about by health care reform has battered the health care stocks since the beginning of 1993. This kind of uncertainty will continue for some time as legislative battles are being fought in the U.S. Congress regarding the health care reform bill. The following trend is clear. More people are switching to HMOs for comprehensive and less costly service. Hospitals are cutting administrative costs, questionable surgery, medical equipment, and inventories of medical supplies. Drug companies are more sensitive to public sentiment when setting prices.

Table 4-10 shows that although the health care profit picture looks good, the stock prices have come down in general. The biggest price drop occurred in the acute care and general hospital services such as Humana and National Medical Enterprise. In addition, the medical equipment companies were also hard hit, such as U.S. Surgical and

Medtronics. Like the drug industry, institutional sponsorship remained about the same, which means the chance of
rebound is great. However, it is advisable to wait until the
uncertainty clears before investing in this industry.

**Table 4-10. Leading Companies in Health Care
and Medical Supplies.**

Company Ranking by 1992 Sales	Profits 1992 ($Mn)	Out-standing Shares (Mn)	Share Prices ($) 1992 High	Apr 93 High	Institution Holdings (%) 1992	1993
Baxtor Intl.	+ 441	277	40 1/2	30 3/8	62	63
Humana	+ 122	159	29 1/2	9 3/8	72	74
Nat.Med. Entpr.	+ 104	166	18 1/8	9 1/8	67	69
Healtrust	- 43	81	23 3/4	17 3/8	n.a.	44
Am.Med.Hldg.	+ 100	77	13	11 1/2	11	34
US Healthcare	+ 200	107	51 1/4	48 1/4	74	74
Medco Contain.	+ 106	152	38 5/8	33	81	86
Pacificare	+ 44	27	51	39	32	16
FHP Intl.	+ 33	33	23	24 3/4	75	71
Caremark Intl.	+ 27	71	15	14 1/8	n.a.	54
United Health.	+ 114	69	58 3/8	55 3/4	84	92
Charter Med.	- 37	25	8 3/4	14 7/8	n.a.	39
US Surgical	+ 139	56	134 1/2	58 3/4	67	63
Medtronic	+ 162	60	104 1/2	75 3/4	70	73

Sources: Fortune Magazine, Standard & Poor's Stock Guide

Utility stocks are considered defensive stocks because
the prices are rather stable despite bad times. Another
reason is the good dividend payments to stockholders.
Institutions invest in utility stocks to keep their portfolios

look good at the bottom line. Since these stocks do not appreciate as much as those in other industries, the percentage of institutional holdings are comparatively low as shown in Table 4-11. Utility companies have large capital outlays, so their long-term debts are high. Interest payments constitute a large portion of operating expenses. Therefore lower interest rates invariably brighten the profit picture of utility companies.

Table 4-11 shows the improved profits of utility companies in 1992. The stock price of AT&T almost doubled between late 1991 and early 1993 as the company returned to high profitability. After divestiture forced by the U.S. Government in 1984, AT&T has seen wide fluctuations in its profits. The company has now evolved into a diversified business with a new focus and ready to exploit the opportunities in worldwide communications.

In recent years, MCI and Sprint have been aggressively pushing into the long-distance phone market held by AT&T in North America. The years ahead will see increasing competition in the world market between these three companies. There will also be alliances with high-tech firms to establish a foothold in the interactive multimedia market which is now taking shape.

Table 4-11. Leading Companies in Utility Industry.

Company Ranking by 1992 Sales	Profits 1992 ($Mn)	Out-standing Shares (Mn)	Share Prices ($) 1992 High	Apr 93 High	Institution Holdings (%) 1992	1993
AT&T	+3807	1340	53 1/8	60 3/8	31	34
GTE	- 754	941	35 3/4	37 3/8	52	49
BellSouth	+1618	494	55 1/2	57	26	26
Bell Atlantic	+1341	432	53 7/8	56 3/8	29	32
US West	- 614	414	40	45	42	42
Nynex	+1311	206	88 1/2	92 1/4	37	39
Pac. Gas&Elec.	+1171	428	34 5/8	35 3/8	37	39
Southwest. Bell	+1302	300	74 3/4	81 1/2	38	39
Ameritech	- 400	270	74	80 1/4	32	32
Pacific Telesis	+1142	404	47	49 1/4	37	38
MCI Comm.	+ 609	262	40 7/8	49 1/4	62	70
Sprint	+ 457	340	26 3/4	33 1/4	n.a.	42

Sources: Fortune Magazine, Standard & Poor's Stock Guide

Stocks of **basic material industries** such as steel, aluminum, paper, wood, glass, etc. usually receive heavy institutional sponsorship because of the values of their inventories. At the beginning of an economic recovery, these stocks rise in anticipation of heavy demands for making finished products. If the economic recovery is slow such as the current one, the stock prices of basic material companies will increase slowly over an extended period.

Foreign competition has hurt some of these industries, especially steel. World price fluctuations of a basic material can have a significant effect on the stock prices of the entire sector. The price of some basic material such as timber will be on the rise due to environmental reasons. This will encourage the use of other materials like plastic and other synthetics as substitutes. Therefore it is difficult to tell the effects on the stock prices of timber companies.

Table 4-12 shows the performance of the basic material companies. The profitability picture is mixed since the economic recovery is still in progress. The stock prices of most major companies have come down from their 1992 levels. However, institutional holdings increase in many cases.

Table 4-12. Leading Companies in Basic Materials Industry.

Company Ranking by 1992 Sales	Profits 1992 ($Mn)	Out- standing Shares (Mn)	Share Prices ($) 1992 High	Apr 93 High	Institution Holdings (%) 1992	1993
Du Pont	-3927	675	54 7/8	53 7/8	40	41
Dow Chemical	- 489	273	62 7/8	56 1/2	50	55
Minn. Mining/Mfg.	+1233	219	85 1/2	116	64	68
Intl. Paper	+ 86	123	78 1/2	67 1/8	65	59
Georgia-Pacific	- 124	88	72	69 1/4	63	65
Aluminum Co.	-1139	86	80 5/8	66 1/2	74	81
Weyerhaeuser	+ 372	208	39 1/4	46 1/2	57	56
Monsanto	- 88	120	71 1/4	56 3/4	63	61
Kimberly-Clark	+ 135	161	63 1/4	55 3/8	69	67
Reynolds Metals	- 749	60	64 3/8	49	75	76
Gillette	+ 513	220	61 1/4	60 5/8	68	72
Bethleham Steel	- 449	91	17 1/4	20	68	78
Crown Cork & Seal	+ 155	89	41 1/8	39 1/2	39	49

Sources: Fortune Magazine, Standard & Poor's Stock Guide

As for the **oil industry,** the price of oil is the most crucial factor. Institutions like to invest in big oil companies because of the good value of oil inventory and the increase in worldwide demand for energy in the long term. Furthermore, oil stocks distribute good dividends like utility stocks. Small oil companies carry great risks because of the initial high capital cost and the precarious nature of oil exploration.

If you like oil stocks, you need to pay attention to the price trend of oil, and the international situation that may affect oil price movements. Like utility companies, oil companies have to finance huge capital expenditures. The reduction of interest rates will improve the profit picture significantly because it brings tremendous savings on interest payments.

The oil industry has been through a slump since the latter half of the 1980s due to the decline of oil prices and reduced consumption. As a result, many companies in the drilling and exploration business were wiped out. With the gradual upturn beginning in 1991, the surviving companies in this business will be able to benefit from increased prices and less competition.

Table 4-13 shows that most major oil companies performed well in 1992. The rise in profits were due to low interest payments and the gradual rise in oil prices. The stock prices have risen somewhat in anticipation of increased demand for energy as a result of the economic recovery.

Table 4-13. Leading Companies in Oil and Oil Products.

Company Ranking by 1992 Sales	Profits 1992 ($Mn)	Out- standing Shares (Mn)	Share Prices ($)		Institution Holdings (%)	
			1992 High	Apr 93 High	1992	1993
Exxon	+4770	1242	65 1/2	69	38	40
Mobil	+ 862	399	69 3/4	71 5/8	55	56
Chevron	+1569	325	75 3/8	86 1/2	42	42
Texaco	+ 712	259	66 7/8	65 3/8	63	63
Amoco	- 74	496	53 3/4	59 1/4	50	55
ARCO	+ 801	159	121 3/4	127 3/4	55	60
USX-Marathon	-1826	287	24 3/4	20 1/8	66	58
Phillips	+ 180	260	28 7/8	31 5/8	43	49

Sources: Fortune Magazine, Standard & Poor's Stock Guide

5 A STRATEGY FOR SMALL INVESTORS

THE RIGHT ATTITUDE

Faced with the preponderant strength of the institutions, the small investors should develop a strategy to enable them to survive and prosper. Let us begin by cultivating the following attitude. First, you should be humble enough to admit that the market can go against you any time in spite of your knowledge, skills and foresight. Therefore, do not allow yourself to be carried away by your judgment and confidence. Second, do not dwell on the past. Look to the future. Never let your past success or failure influence your decision to go into a stock. Each batch of investment is unique because of changing circumstances. Thus it has to be viewed objectively. Third, keep an open mind but do not get swayed by other people's opinions.

I used to think of a small investor like myself as a surfer. The surfboard is my capital. The sea is the stock market. The incoming waves are the never-ending stream of opportunities. I have heard that a certain beach is good for surfing. So I take the trouble of going there. I paddle out to the sea in the hope of getting a great fun. I am taking some risk now because a shark may appear out of nowhere, but I cannot worry too much about it. I know I can do absolutely nothing about the waves. Neither do I want to predict when a good wave will come. I will ride it when I see a good one. Many waves have passed me by. They turn out to be good but I did not see them at that time. So I just continue to wait and see. Sooner or later I will be able to catch a good wave. I play my best with the surfing skills I have learned. The wave takes me back to the beach. I have had a lot of fun. With each ride, good or bad, I learn something new. I am prepared to go out again for some more rides. I hope that the readers will appreciate this analogy.

PATIENCE BEFORE COMMITMENT

Just like the stream of never-ending waves hitting the beach, the opportunities of the stock market pass you by everyday. However, this does not mean that you should get in right away. You know that with limited financial resources, you are going to miss the great majority of them anyway. Why should that bother you? Remember the surfer out there? You need a lot of patience to wait, hear and see before you jump in. You want to be reasonably sure that you have found a good one. Never let yourself be pushed into a stock because of the anxiety that you may miss the boat. In fact, there are hundreds of them waiting for you everyday, more than you will ever know. Why put yourself in such a hurry?

The most important element in your investment strategy is patience, especially before you get into the market. With cash in your hand protected by your patience, you have total control of your fate. Once you are in, you turn over control to the ups and downs of the market. Your patience then becomes a two-edge sword. If you have bought a stock which is due to rise in a matter of months, your patience will help you survive any temporary setbacks and will eventually pay off. On the other hand, if you have made a bad investment choice, your patience buoyed by hope will urge you to wait for an upturn when you see the stock price tumbling. Eventually you wake up to the realities and painfully take a loss. What it boils down to is everyday common sense. That is when you do things, take the time to evaluate and plan, then most things will turn out all right despite some initial hardships.

PRICE ILLUSIONS

While patience lies within you, the price of a stock is something external that can get you into trouble. It is only natural for people to think that a lower price is cheap so the stock is worth buying. When the price is beckoning you, your patience should come to your rescue. You should never buy a stock when the price continues falling because you never know when the institutions are done with unloading.

Time is the ultimate test for the bottom or support price of a stock. When a stock hits the bottom, it tends to stay there for quite some time before it has a chance to pick up. Sometimes it will never pick up at all. You have to find out the reasons for its descent. If it is market uncertainties, wait for the clouds to clear. If it is earnings related, wait for a couple of quarterly reports to verify a sustainable recovery.

Conversely, there is temptation to sell a stock when it reaches a certain high price. In this situation, you are under much less pressure because your cost is below the market value. It may not be a bad idea to cash out soon, because you can move on to another company, or come back to the same one when the price has dropped after you cashed out. If you choose to stick with the stock, you may have the chance for a bonanza that comes later with stock splits and further price increases, or you may stand to lose what you have gained so far. There is a way to insure against this risk which will be discussed later.

In order to make a profit in a business, you have to buy low and sell high. This may not be true for stocks. Suppose you buy 100 shares of a company at $40 per share. Your total cost is $4,000 ignoring the commission. After two months the price still stays about the same, but the stock has split. Thus you now own 200 shares at $20 per share. Another two months elapse and the stock price goes up to $25. You sell all the stocks for a total of $5,000, thereby making a profit of $1,000 discounting the commissions. You have bought high at $40 and sold low at $25 and still made a good profit. The obvious reason is the earning power of a stock split. This shows that the price of a stock should not be over-emphasized in your investment decisions because other factors often take on greater importance. You should never assume that the price of a stock represents the company's worth. In the stock market, worth is only in the eyes of the big beholders, which are the institutional investors. As a matter of fact, the stock price is all phony and fake. When a company goes public, the investment bankers have agreed to supply money to the company and float the new shares. The finance capital depends on the number of shares issued and the agreed price per share. Some mutual funds may also be asked to participate with the investment bankers. This is the primary financial market where the company obtains financing from the investment bankers and mutual funds.

On the day of initial public offering (IPO), the investment bankers float the shares at the IPO price to the stock market which is in fact the secondary financial market. The public is then allowed to purchase, and the stock price is left to the market mechanism of supply and demand. On that day, the company has already received the financing it needs. If the stock price goes up in frenzied buying usually characteristic of an IPO, the investment bankers and the participating mutual funds will have recouped all of their investments after they sell the new shares for the first time. In effect, money flows from the public via the investment bankers to the company. From that time onward, the stock price has a dynamics of its own in the marketplace and has little to do with financing the company. When the stock market is hot, companies will find it easier to obtain financing from investment bankers who can recover their investments quickly through stock offerings in the secondary financial market.

To see why stock prices are phony, just imagine that the stock market shuts down for an indefinite period, or everybody refuses to buy stocks. Where should the stock prices be? There would be either no prices or zero prices. Would this affect the performance of public companies? Not at all! Life will go on as usual. People still go to the banks, borrow money to buy houses and cars, and consume food and clothing. Companies continue to produce to satisfy consumer demands. Companies can prove their real worth by generating incomes and making profits.

Stock prices cannot affect the operations of public companies, hence their true worth. The same can be said after a stock market crash, which hurts the investors but can do little to hamper the operations of the business world. The stock market only reflects the state of the economy and the mood of the investors. The bull can never hope to pull the economy out of a recession, nor can the bear hope to suppress consumer demands. On the other hand, if the world goes into a deep recession, the stock market is the first one to suffer.

DIVERSIFICATION OR CONCENTRATION?

Mutual funds diversify to protect themselves and to make a selling point regarding the security of their assets. Should you as a small investor diversify? You do not need to. The first thing to consider is the affordability of diversification. Most small investors have a limited budget to invest. Maintaining a diversity of stocks means holding a very small quantity for each. Too small a quantity requires a large price difference to make the profit significant. In addition, there is the cost of brokers' commissions which eat into your profits. Diversification does not offer the potential of big killings. Suppose you have bought a stock that has risen twice as much and is due to split. Wouldn't you like to have invested every single penny in it?

Small investors should cultivate an interest in a diversity of stocks including non-favorite industries and companies. After all, if a company's stock helps you make a profit, why should you be fussy about its products or anything else? If you are tracking the stock performance of say 20 to 30 companies across all industries, you will have availed yourself of a wider range of opportunities. The institutional investors like to move money from one industry to another. Limiting your eyesight on your favorite industry means that you have to wait for the next cycle to come around. In short, you should diversify your interests, but concentrate your investment once you have spotted a good opportunity.

THE GRANDMOTHER'S APPROACH

The easiest and most enjoyable way to invest is the grandmother's method. All you need is faith in the capitalist system and in corporate America. Remember what my grandma did as described in Chapter 4? When you invest for the long term, you rid yourself of all the anxieties of daily ups and downs, even temporary crashes. You can even shut yourself from the daily bombardment of confusing information from professionals and other sources. The long term does not mean 15 to 30 years like the mortgage on a house. In just a few years' time, great profits can be realized for so-called long-term investments in stocks.

If you want to take the grandmother approach, it is safer to avoid high-tech industries which are prone to product revolutions due to technological breakthroughs. A high-tech company is constantly under siege because technology is developing in an ever faster pace. Externally, a high-tech company faces fierce competition. Internally, it faces obsolescense of its machinery, and perhaps the inertia and complacency of management which render the company unable to adapt to changing market conditions. The consequence is wide fluctuations for high-tech stocks.

The grandmother approach requires investment in stable industries with long-term growth prospects such as food, beverages, soaps, clothing, body-care products, drugs, utilities, and oil as discussed in Chapter 4. The leading American companies in these industries are excellent candidates for investment. Their names you can see or hear everyday in homes, supermarkets, restaurants and shopping centers.

THE INVESTIGATION PROCESS

If you are not convinced about the wisdom of the grandmother approach, you may like to adopt a sophisticated method based on analysis rather than faith. Where do you begin? Well, you pick the companies of interest, the stocks that capture your attention for whatever reason, or the recommendations from friends, analysts or the media. It should be emphasized that all the company names you obtain can serve as leads only for further investigations. You may wind up investing in one or more of those leads, or discarding all of them.

It is wise to allocate a fixed budget for stock investment. You must always resist the temptation to increase the budget unless some extra money comes along that you do not need for daily expenses. You should never buy stocks with your salary because when you need the money, the stock price always goes down.

Now you start accumulating a list of companies from different sources. What should your objective be? The bottom line is that you want to find some certainty regarding the direction of the stock price in the medium to long term, that is three months or longer. If you are not able to see any price certainty in a stock, you should not bet on it. You must not subject yourself to pure luck by betting. Always remember that you are a small investor. You want to find a stock favored by the institutions, not by yourself.

While researching into your list of companies, you should strive to be objective and concentrate on the most relevant information. The common sources of information include: company financial reports, newspapers, financial journals, and brokerage houses. Major newspapers and financial journals are available in local community libraries. You may also like to subscribe to a personal computer network program currently available.

During your investigation, you should gather the following information:

- *Earnings change from one quarter to the next.* This shows if the company can keep up with previous records of performance. Changes in the existing pattern can signal a price movement. By comparing the current quarter with the previous one, and also with the same quarter of the previous year, you can see how the pattern looks like. Earnings change from a big loss to a small gain usually has greater effect on the stock price than successive small gains which tend to raise investors' expectations. Remember the changes in earnings are more important than the absolute figures. The common sources of data are: company reports, Investor's Business Daily, or your broker.

- *Number of shares outstanding.* This has a lot to do with the potential for price rise and stock splits. A smaller number is always better. View this in relation to the price range of previous years. Also compare with a company of similar size and in the same industry. The latest figures can be obtained from Standard & Poor's Stock Guide published monthly.

- *Changes in institutional holdings.* This shows if the big investors' commitments in the stock have changed. Try to reason why if you find a significant change. The latest figures can be obtained from Standard & Poor's Stock Guide published monthly. It is safe to avoid a stock when you see institutional holdings decline in parallel with a price drop.

- *Stock price and volume.* You should track the price movement of the stock and associated volume of trade on a daily basis. For a rising stock, the down days usually show a smaller volume of trade than the up days. If you care to total the up volumes and the down volumes for a week or two, you will get some idea about how many more shares have been purchased to cause the price increase. The data can be obtained from daily newspapers or financial journals.

- *Changes in company cash holding and long-term debt.* This is important when you consider buying a stock at a low price level. If the company concerned

has a small cash holding left and the long-term debt
has increased, it may be a candidate for bankruptcy.
The latest figures can be obtained from Standard &
Poor's Stock Guide published monthly.

- *Quarterly changes in sales.* This is more important
  for small companies than for big ones. Growth
  companies are characterized by a string of big
  increases of sales in parallel with profits. The
  common sources of data are: company reports,
  Investor's Business Daily, or your broker.

- *Date of next quarterly earnings release.* This can be
  obtained by calling the Investor Relations Office of
  the company concerned. The market reaction on the
  first few days after the release usually determines the
  course of the stock price in the next three months.

- *Significant news.* You should pay attention to daily
  news which can affect the stock price. Try to develop
  the ability to separate the most relevant news from
  the rest. Also observe the market reaction for the first
  few days after the news to verify its importance. The
  most relevant piece of news that always affects the
  stock price is about pricing. It is not abnormal to see
  the stock price plunging ten to twenty percent in one
  day when a company announces a price cut of a
  major product. Besides the short-term effect, price
  cutting is likely to reduce the profits of the company

in the longer term if bigger sales volumes cannot be generated to compensate for it.

• *P/E ratio.* Get the P/E ratio of the stock from the Wall Street Journal or Investor's Business Daily, and compare it with that of the S&P 500 Index. Also compare it with similar companies of the same industry. This will show how much the current stock price is out of line with the rest.

• *Non-recurrent charges.* Find out if there are any one-time charges for the current quarter or the next in the company's financial report. These charges include: merger cost, loss writeoff, restructuring charge, etc. The inclusion or disappearance of these charges usually skews the earnings of the company thus affecting the stock price.

• *Non-recurrent income.* Sometimes a company may have struck a deal to sell an unprofitable division for a large sum of money. This sale will increase the company's cash holdings and its earnings for the next few quarters. There will also be savings in operating costs due to the transfer of the unprofitable division. The stock price usually rises in expectation of better earnings to come.

• *Any less significant information.* You may like to add some more things to investigate if time permits. Whatever you do, be sure to ask how much net effect there will be on the quarterly earnings and whether the institutions will likely be impressed.

- *Short list of stocks.* You will eventually come up with a short list of companies for investment. Try to rank the companies based on the results of the investigation. From this list you will pick the best ones according to the size of your budget. You may also like to cash out some of your existing holdings if the investigation does not show good prospects for those companies. Remember that you undertake this effort to find some stocks for investment in the medium to long term, that is three months or longer.

PLAY THE REBOUND

Since your objective is to look for some certainty in the direction of stock price movement, the most obvious certainty that happens all the time is the rebound of big companies. You shoud build a list of big companies that have hit a low price for your own investigation. The reasons for big company rebound have been discussed in Chapter 3. The bull market that began in the winter of 1991 has fostered the rebound of many big companies whose earnings are sensitive to interest rate reductions and the general economic recovery. These include Citicorp, Chrysler, and Goodyear Tire. They are now moving in a cyclical fashion after the rebound.

There is a second kind of big company rebound due to non-recurrent charges. At any time of the year you will find some stocks of big companies hitting the bottom due to declining earnings. If the negative earnings are the results of restructuring or merger costs, there will be a significant improvement once those non-recurrent charges are out of the way even without revenue increase. So you need to include those companies in the list for further investigation. Some examples are IBM and Digital Equipment.

The third kind of big company rebound occurs in areas where uncertainty sets in. The health care reform program initiated by the Clinton Administration has caused many casualties in the health care, medical, and drug industries in early 1993. Many stocks have been battered just because they happened to be in the industry, not because of bad earnings. When the uncertainty begins to clear, those stocks will probably move back to the original levels. Some examples include Humana, U.S. Surgical, Medtronics, Merck and Amgen. A recent uncertainty precipitated by Philip Morris concerns the future of brand names for the consumer industry. You may like to include the affected companies in your investigation for the likelihood of a later rebound. So add Philip Morris and other big brand names to your investigation list.

There is a fourth kind of big company rebound. In this case, the big companies have incurred great losses for a couple of years but are now gradually recovering. The earnings improvement due to restructuring have already sent the stock price higher. The next thing to watch out for is revenue growth and resumption of dividends. If that happens, the stock will recapture its glorious past. Some examples are Unisys and National Semiconductors.

The fifth kind of big company rebound involves divestiture. Many giant American companies suddenly discover that they have grown too big and diverse, to the extent of having a negative effect on profitability. As a consequence these companies are planning to sell some of their unprofitable subsidiaries. We have already seen the divestiture effect on the stock price of General Dynamics in 1992. You should add the following companies to your investigation list: Sears, American Express, and Eastman Kodak.

The sixth kind of big company rebound comes only once a while, which involves a crash, some shocking news, or a war. You probably remember the depressing and rebounding effects of the Persian Gulf War in early 1991. You can take advantage of these temporary dips if you have some surplus cash ready. As you can see, opportunities abound in the stock market. They come and go all year round. That is why cultivating patience before commitment is important. You need to have the cash ready and wait for a good one to come by. There are enough opportunities already just by concentrating on the big companies.

For medium to small companies, the rebound is less certain and depends on more factors. Because these companies have less fats and wastes, there is a limit to how much they can save by restructuring. Therefore, they definitely need a revenue boost to cause a rebound. Some companies may not even make it to rebound if their cash holdings are too small to help them pull through the difficult period.

Since a small company is seldom in the core portfolio of institutional investors as discussed in Chapter 3, it is difficult to find out where the lowest support price is. To buy into a small company at a low price presents more risks. Therefore the best way is to wait until you see a sustainable upturn supported by increased sales and profits. This waiting period usually lasts for several months when the stock price settles down to the lowest level. Once again, you should not worry about missing the boat. It is better missing the initial price increase than getting into an unsustainable rebound.

If you remember the biotech craze back in 1991, do you think it will return? Why not? The biotech field is a precious American jewel still in its infancy and protected by patents. Investors do not have to be impressed by present earnings to appreciate the great potential of their research work. The revival of the biotech craze depends on the performance of other industries. Up to mid-1993, high-tech companies seem to have captured the limelight. There will be a time when most of the stocks across all industries are relatively low and flat, and interest rates stay low resulting in plenty of cash floating around. Then some big investors will trumpet and push the biotech companies again. So make sure you don't miss the boat next time.

PLAY THE CYCLICAL MOVEMENT

When a stock completes a rebound, it will stay at a higher level and move in an up-and-down cyclical fashion. This is the period where most uncertainties exist. When you go into the cyclical phase, you are subject to all kinds of developments that can influence the stock price. You need quite a bit of luck to come out a winner. Because of daily changing circumstances, you are forced to play the short term and keep track of current developments on a daily basis.

There are some exceptions such as utility and big oil companies where fewer disturbances can knock them out of the cyclical orbit. On the positive side, some cyclical stocks succeed moving onto a higher plane. Intel is a good example whose price ran up from around $60 to $110 between late1992 and early 1993. On the negative side, Philip Morris was knocked out of its higher cyclical orbit at around $70 to a lower $48 in just a single day in early April 1993.

If you do not mind playing the cyclical phase, you should minimize the risk by concentrating on growth companies. Growth companies usually find themselves steadily rising from one cyclical pattern to a higher one until they finally stabilize. The stabilization comes when the revenue increase finally slows down, or when the shares outstanding reach a big quantity due to successive splits. After that it will take a huge sum of money to buy up the price with so many shares outstanding.

There are always growth companies around that capture your attention. You have to really see their performance in the stock market before you invest in them. The key is patience again. One or two quarters of good performance are not enough. Only the cream of the crop can make sustainable growth. In the early 1990s, computer network and database software have taken the spotlight. Notable examples are Novell, Cisco, Cabletron, SynOptics, Oracle, Sybase and Informix. These companies have brought high returns to investors during the period between 1991 and 1992. If you happen to be in these companies, you will have to find out when the stabilization phase is likely to arrive by investigating the pace of revenue and earning increases and the quantity of shares issued.

INSURING YOUR INVESTMENTS

With limited budget, a small investor faces a difficult position after buying into the wrong stock. To get out means a financial loss. To stay put means tying up your money and missing some other opportunities. If you see no prospect for an upturn soon, it will be wise to sell and get out. The best position for a small investor is to have the cash in hand. You should never sink more money into a falling stock by adopting the cost averaging method. If you want cost averaging, why not wait until the stock has sunk to the lowest level? Suppose you get to the lowest level, how long will it take before a rebound can occur? What is the probability that the company is heading toward bankruptcy?

If you have bought the right stock, there is little pressure to sell as the price is rising. Normally, there are two considerations: when to take the profit and get out, and whether to buy some more for additional gains. It is up to the individual to decide depending on the objective and the circumstances that may change the objective. However, there is a third consideration, that is to guarantee your gain while you take the time to decide what to do. The following diagram illustrates:

——————————— $35 Market price[1]

——————————— $30 Sell short 100 shares, February 1993

——————————— $25 Market price[2]

——————————— $20 Buy long 100 shares, January 1993

——————————— $10 Market price[3]

In the above diagram, suppose you maintain two positions in your trading account. The first position was established when you bought 100 shares of a stock at $20 per share. One month later when the price has gone up to $30 you established the second position by selling short the same amount. Selling short means you sell to your brokerage firm without actually owning the stock. In other words, you owe your brokerage firm the stock which you will have to buy back later at the going market price. In this particular case, you own the stock but you do not want to give it up, so you sell short. You will find that your gain of $10 per share will be guaranteed no matter where the market price moves. Let us work out the details:

When market price is $35, liquidate both positions
Gain from buy long, $35x100 - $20x100 = $1500
Loss from sell short, $35x100 - $30x100 = $ 500
Therefore, net gain equals $1000

When market price is $25, liquidate both positions
Gain from buy long, $25x100 - $20x100 = $ 500
Gain from sell short, $30x100 - $25x100 = $ 500
Therefore, net gain equals $1000

When market price is $10, liquidate both positions
Loss from buy long, $20x100 - $10x100 = $1000
Gain from sell short, $30x100 - $10x100 = $2000
Therefore, net gain equals $1000

By repeating the above calculations, you will also find that regardless of the market price, your gain is dependent on the gap between the buy long price and the sell short price. If you manage to increase this gap continuously, you can guarantee a bigger and bigger gain on the same stock.

What is the maintenance cost for two positions? Suppose you open a margin account which normally requires a deposit in cash of 50 percent of the market value of the stock. In this example, your first position (buy long of 100 shares at $20 per share) requires $1000 cash already paid. Your second position (sell short of 100 shares at the current market price of $30) should require an extra $1500. However, you do not have to pay this much extra cash due to the appreciation of your first position from $2000 to $3000. Based on this market value, your broker considers you to have $1500 cash rather than $1000 which you actually put in. Therefore, the broker is prepared to lend you $500 which can be used to pay for the short requirement. Thus the additional cash you have to pay for the second position is $1500-$500=$1000. Based on this calculation, you will find that no matter how high the market price goes, you only need to double your original cash to insure your first position. In this example, you pay $1000 to insure your first position.

To carry this example further, suppose you opened the first buy long position of 1000 shares at $20 per share. When the price rises to $30, the value of your investment has appreciated by $10,000. Your broker is prepared to lend you $5000. If you do not wish to insure the whole investment, you can just do part of it by short selling say 300 shares at $30. This requires only $4,500 cash which can be financed out of the appreciation on your first position. This means that you do not have to pay any extra cash to insure 300 out of your 1000 shares. Some brokers may have a smaller cash requirement for selling short a stock which you already own. In that case, it will cost even less to insure your investments.

There are many ways to play the insurance game by moving just one position based on the direction of the current market price. This game is most suitable for stocks in the cyclical phase. You continue to play until the time is ripe to get out of the stock altogether. Then you just liquidate both positions. Let us use the previous example:

_____	$35 Market price ^{2}
_____	$30 Sell short 100 shares, February 1993
_____	$25 Market price^1
_____	$20 Buy long 100 shares, January 1993
_____	$10 Market price^3

Suppose you have installed both positions at $20 and $30. When the price rises to $35, you may like to do nothing because you anticipate it will drop. When the price comes down to $25, if you think it will rebound, then you liquidate the sell short and pocket the $5 per share gain. When the price goes back up to $35, you sell short again.

This time you manage to increase the gap between the buy long and sell short postions. When you see some signs that the stock is in for a continuous slide, you liquidate the buy long position first to pocket the gain of $35-$20=$15 per share. Then you wait for the slide to go further. Finally, you liquidate the short sell position when the price comes down to $10. Your gain is then $35-$10=$25 per share.

The aforementioned example is of course an ideal situation. The stock price seldom moves the way you expect it to. The point is that this insurance scheme guarantees your gain and gives you time to decide what to do. With some luck and sophistication, you may be able to reap some short-term benefits by liquidating one position after another at the appropriate times.

In this insurance scheme, short selling is used to insure the buy long, and vice versa. Under normal conditions, it is more risky to sell short on a stock unless the company is heading toward bankruptcy. Theoretically speaking, when you buy long, the most you can lose is when the stock price goes down to zero. When you sell short, there is no limit for your loss because the price can go up and up, and the stock can split and split. Worse still, your short sell enters into the records of your brokerage firm. Together with other short sells, it will be available on public records as an aggregrate number. The institutional investors know about this. Unless the stock's decline is impossible to arrest, the institutions may move the price up and benefit at your expense.

SOME MARKET OBSERVATIONS

Small investors are always advised to set your sight on the medium or long term to eliminate the agony and confusion of daily price movements. However, observations about short term price movements are helpful when you want to gain a couple of points here and there to pay for brokers' commissions.

When the release date of quarterly earnings approaches, the stock usually gets jittery due to investors' anxiety. The price normally moves either up or down for a number of days right up to the release date. If it moves up, chances are the earnings will cause a price drop after release. If it comes down, chances are the earnings release will boost up the price. The readers are encouraged to pick a few stocks and verify their observations.

This is really a strange but consistent phenomenon. It fuels speculation about leaks of quarterly earnings. Leaks are facts of life which we should be aware of. Confidential information has leaked from the White House or the U.S. Congress from time to time. Even military secrets have leaked from the Pentagon or the CIA. Why should the stock market be any different?

Another observation is the price fluctuation during a trading day. If a stock is due to go up on a particular day, the price usually dips during the first hour of trading. Then it picks up steadily and reaches a higher point when the market closes. The reverse is also true for a stock due to come down. This pattern is broken when significant news about the stock arrives during the trading day. Small investors are urged to verify this market observation.

There is an easy explanation for this price movement. When a mutual fund decides to add say 100,000 shares of a stock to its existing holding, to start the purchase early in the morning when people are less ready to sell will raise the price too quickly. It is better to dump 20,000 of its existing holding in the first hour to depress the price and encourage some sellers, then start buying 120,000 later in the day. The same reasoning applies when a mutual fund decides to reduce its existing holding of a stock.

6 CONCLUSION

The stock market is an exciting place to be in when there are price movements. All investors have to count on prices to move, otherwise nobody will be able to make a profit. Of course, everyone wants prices to move in the preferred directions, but only the big price movers can make it happen. The price movers are the institutional investors. They trade in high volumes on a daily basis, and generate waves after waves by moving money from one industry or company to another. The small investors are always playing catchups in this game.

The waves are created for various reasons depending on the market situation and opportunies elsewhere. However, the bottom line is the profitability of the company. A company that stays in the red will eventually be deserted by investors. Small investors should realize that in the medium to long run, good earnings will invariably lead to higher stock prices. In the short term however, it all depends on how the institutions view the stocks in relation to other opportunities.

There are thousands of ways to select stocks for investment. This book emphasizes on the very fundamentals. Small investors should try to visualize institutional behavior with respect to the stocks they are interested in. The question often asked about a stock is: "What kinds of product does the company make?". Although this is important, it does not get to the heart of the investment investigation. The question should be: "How much profit is the company making? And does it satisfy the institutional investors?".

There is no need for lengthy company or product research to identify good stocks. Only a few basic figures will do. In short, small investors should try to swim with the waves created by institutional investors. Trying to predict the waves most likely results in half of the time being right and half being wrong. Why should one bother with that? Small investors should only go into a stock when they see much better than a 50 percent chance of success. With limited financial resources, small investors must play defensively to conserve capital. They must cultivate a broad interest in all types of industries to avail themselves of a greater opportunity. Once a decision is made, they should concentrate investments in a few companies to reap the most benefit.

Small investors must realize that of the huge pool of information available to them, only a minute portion is directly relevant to the stock price movement. They must learn how to distill the very fundamental data that point to the future movement of the stock price. They have to view things in the medium to long term, because those things can be foreseen with reasonable certainty by relying on the fundamental data available. Playing the short term means following the whims of the institutional investors, which is too chancy and therefore risky.

One obvious certainty is the rebound of big companies which are leaders in their respective industries. These companies are favored by institutional investors for long-term security. They have heavy institutional sponsorship which are unlikely to evaporate in a short period. Thus small investors have plenty of time to get out when a crisis appears.

During down times, the stock prices of big companies normally come down gradually and settle to a lower level. This is known as the support level which is relatively easy to identify. To take advantage of the rebound, small investors should try to move into this low level when the worst appears to be over. After the rebound, these companies will be moving in their normal cyclical orbits. There will be higher risks playing in the cyclical phase than the rebound phase.

On the other hand, smaller companies usually do not receive long-term institutional sponsorship. Therefore, as institutional money comes and goes, the stock prices follow a volatile pattern. It is rather difficult to find a support price level for these companies. There probably exist equal amounts of benefit and risk associated with investing in these companies. Small investors should exercise more caution when playing these stocks.

Growth companies belong to a different breed of smaller companies. During the initial stages, a growth company experiences a lot of difficulties and uncertainties. Small investors should allow time for a growth company to prove itself in the marketplace and to attract the sponsorship of institutional investors. After a few quarters of good earnings, the stock price of a growth company will rise rapidly and continue to break previous record highs as more and more institutions are moving in. It is not late for the small investors to cash in at this time. The bonanza for a successful growth company usually comes one or two years later with stock splits and further price increases. It is better to miss the initial stages of growth than to get into a company that fizzles.

Apart from financial resources, institutional investors possess huge advantages over small investors in the kind of trading information they can obtain. Most small investors are too carried away by the technical data disseminated from the institutions. They are willing to accept that those technical information will give them an edge to win. How can they win if the big players are holding all the good cards in the game?

To make the stock game more fair, small investors should form an alliance to push for more security exchange regulations requiring institutions to reveal more about their trading practices and sponsorship of public companies.

Exactly what kind of information that the public wants will require further studies. However, the following deserves some consideration.

The institutions should regularly reveal the quantities of shares they own in all public companies and the average costs of their holdings with respect to each company. The public also wants to know the percentage of institutional trading of a given stock for each trading day. These are two examples showing institutional commitments which influence prices most significantly.

The stock market is tilted too heavily in favor of the institutions. While too many restricting rules can choke off the stock market, more revelations on the part of the institutions can only result in a fairer trading environment. It is now time for the small investors to demand more fairness in the stock market.

MORE GREAT READING!

DE THE WAVES by John Fung. No one is able to correctly predict stock arket trends all of the time. Therefore, an investor must have a good strategy to rvive and to prosper. This straightforward book helps the small investor to estigate market trends and to formulate a strategy for success.

0.95   ISBN 1-56875-075-7   Order #075-7

E MONEY ENGINE by Andrian Kremm. If you've ever wanted to make ney in the stock market without having to depend on luck, this book will show u how. Based on new insights into the buy low and sell high concept, this book ows you a simple method of investing that you can drive to the bank.

.95   ISBN 0-88247-957-1   Order #957-1

E TAO OF GOLF by Leland T. Lewis. Why do the greatest golfers all seem to y with such effortless grace? They have mastered the Tao, or inner game of f. The Tao is the balance of Yin and Yang, masculine and feminine, active and active principles that rule the Universe. **This book goes beyond golf and will instructive to others, as well as golfers.**

95   ISBN 0-88247-923-7   Order #923-7

E WINNING FEELING by John R. Kearns and Garry Shulman. Champion letes know how to get that "winning feeling" on command. Two educators who coach Olympic athletes have created a new system to help students win in classroom. This book will help teachers and parents to instill self-confidence competence in students of all ages.

95   ISBN 1-56875-060-9   Order #060-9

E JOY OF JOB HUNTING by Joseph Bisignano. When interviewing for a job, there is a crucial 15 second period that can make or break your chances. rn the real do's and don'ts of finding and landing a new job. People who follow se rules can rise to the top. Those who violate them won't even get in the front r.

35   ISBN 1-56875-054-4   Order #054-4

THE LEADERSHIP HANDBOOK: 101 Ways to be a Super-Leader and Avoid Self-Destructio by Will Clark. The Leadership Handbook will teach everyone in the business world and in th private sector how to lead effectively. It will show the reader what gets results, what to avoid, ho to motivate someone or an entire organization, how to solve problems, use effectiv communications, how to form real power, and how to gain respect of your fellow associates in ar kind of situation.

| $14.95 | LC 91-61312 | ISBN 0-88247-874 |
| Softcover | 6x9 | Order #874 |

THE PRESENTATION HANDBOOK: How to Prepare Dynamic Technical and Non-Technic Presentations by John Carrington-Musci. The ability to make effective presentations becoming increasingly important for career advancement. Now there is a book that can help you make winning presentations. The Presentation Handbook can reduce the fear of makir presentations while providing a system of gathering and presenting material that can be used any situation.

| $14.95 | LC 91-61314 | ISBN 0-88247-872 |
| Trade Paper | 6x9 | Order #872 |

THE SOLUTION STRATEGY: Your Handbook for Solving Life's Problems by P McWilliams. If you didn't have any problems, what would you do? You'd probably be reading T Solution Strategy by Phil McWilliams. He has written the one book you need to solve any proble Now you can stop relying on luck or guesswork to handle difficult situations. With this step-by-st technique you'll be able to determine where your problems come from, how to identify them a then—eliminate them. You'll learn how to overcome problems through the integration of emotic and intellect. Once you learn these techniques, you'll be able to accomplish any goal. T Solution Strategy is not Pop Psychology or Religion. It is a new kind of self-help book that re works!